THE MAJOR
THE LIFE AND TIMES OF FRANK BUCKLEY

THE MAJOR
THE LIFE AND TIMES OF FRANK BUCKLEY

PATRICK A. QUIRKE

TEMPUS

Front cover illustration: Major Frank Buckley in his trademark flat cap and plus fours at Molineux in the 1930s.

Back cover illustration: Major Buckley instructing his young Wolves players.

First published 2006

Tempus Publishing Limited
The Mill, Brimscombe Port,
Stroud, Gloucestershire, GL5 2QG
www.tempus-publishing.com

© Patrick A. Quirke, 2006

The right of Patrick A. Quirke to be identified as the Author
of this work has been asserted in accordance with the
Copyrights, Designs and Patents Act 1988.

British Library Cataloguing in Publication Data.
A catalogue record for this book is available from the British Library.

ISBN 0 7524 3606 6

Typesetting and origination by Tempus Publishing Limited
Printed in Great Britain

CONTENTS

	Introduction	8
One	A Soldier, and the Son of a Soldier	9
Two	The Wandering Minstrel	25
Three	The Great International	35
Four	Tangerines and Golf!	52
Five	Waking the Wolf	68
Six	Dances at Wolves	80
Seven	After the Dance	101
Eight	In the Land of the Giants	123
Nine	In the Laboratory of Some Mad Professor	132

With thanks to Wolverhampton Wanderers F.C; their
historian Graham Hughes and to Mrs Wendi Friend, the
Major's great neice.

INTRODUCTION

In the 1950s everyone knew of the famous 'Busby Babes' of Manchester United. The achievements of these talented players and their management became a sporting legend. However, the team that Matt Busby built at Old Trafford were not the first to be christened 'Babes'.

A generation before, Wolverhampton Wanderers had fielded a team of 'Babes' – young and gifted players who were on the verge of great success, only to be thwarted by the outbreak of the Second World War. These were the 'Buckley Babes'. Among their ranks were Stan Cullis and Billy Wright, destined to take their rightful places in the Football Hall of Fame, while later discoveries included the great John Charles of Leeds and Juventus. They all owed their success and achievements to one inspirational and farsighted man, Major Frank Buckley.

Born in the backstreets of late Victorian Manchester, Buckley initially followed his father into the Army. He later plied his trade as a footballer at clubs around the country at a time when the game was being established as the most significant sport in the land.

Representing England in one of the last international matches before the First World War, Buckley was to learn the skills of man-management, tactics and innovation in the battle-torn trenches of the Somme. Although badly wounded in action, he went on to establish the concept of the football manager recognisable today.

Major Buckley has been entitled the 'star maker', 'ultimate publicist', the 'monkey gland manager' and 'football's iron man'. His story is both amazing and full of incident, but despite such titles being given him he will always be – first and foremost – The Major!

ONE

A SOLDIER, AND THE
SON OF A SOLDIER

Franklin Charles Buckley was born at 51 Highfield Terrace, Westbourne Road in Urmston, Lancashire on 3 October 1882, although he always believed his date of birth was 9 November that year. His father, John Buckley, who hailed from the city of Cork, was born into a soldiering family and followed a long tradition of Irishmen serving in Queen Victoria's Army. John Buckley had been a regular soldier in the British Army for a number of years by the time Franklin (or 'Frank' as he was to become better known) was born.

In 1869, at the age of seventeen, John Buckley had left his job as a silk worker in Cork and had travelled to Stockport in Lancashire where he enlisted in the Army. He originally joined the 1st Battalion of an infantry regiment known as 'the King's' (originally called 'The 8th of Foot'). Within a year he had transferred to its sister battalion, the 2nd. He was an exceptionally good soldier and within eight years had risen through the ranks to be promoted to Sergeant. He was to serve as a regular soldier for over twenty years and gained a number of good conduct medals. He was awarded a silver medal for good conduct and long service in 1880.

There is some dispute about where Frank's mother Julia came from. Census records state that she was born in Maidstone, Kent, but on her marriage certificate she claims to have been born in Macclesfield in Cheshire. Julia Buckley's maiden name was Franklin. Following an established Victorian practice whereby the mother's maiden name was given to one of her children so that it did not die out upon her marriage, John and Julia christened their sixth child of eight Franklin, giving him a rather distinctive Christian name.

The eldest Buckley child was some thirteen years older than Frank. The birthplaces of the children reflect the frequency and nature of John Buckley's British or 'Home' postings, although he had served the Empire overseas during the course of his military career. His battalion (the 2nd Battalion of the 8th of Foot Regiment) had served on British island colonies in the Mediterranean during the 1860s and in fact

Westbourne Road, Urmston – Franklin Buckley's birthplace.

A Private of the 8th of Foot, c. 1863. (C. Cougan Military Pictures)

John and Julia Buckley had a military wedding at Floriana Barracks on Malta in late October 1867. Successfully obtaining permission to marry from the commanding officer again indicated the high regard his superiors had for John Buckley. 'Other rank' marriages were not encouraged by the Army at that time, as taking a soldier's family on tours of duty around the Empire was burdensome. Only a limited number of 'steady' men like John Buckley were allowed to wed. His bride, Julia, who was most likely a maidservant to an officer's family, lied about her age so that parental permission for her marriage did not have to be sought. Nevertheless it was to be a successful and long-lasting marriage, with the couple being together for forty years.

After a first year of married life living in an Army bell tent, the Buckleys returned with the regiment to Aldershot Barracks where Julia gave birth to the first of her children, whom they christened Benjamin after Julia's father.

Over the course of the next decade the battalion had a number of postings, including Cork in Ireland as well as regular stints at Aldershot in Hampshire. Having had three children in quick succession while stationed in England, it was while in Ireland that the Buckleys had their fourth and fifth children, Mary Elizabeth in 1873 and Mathew in 1876. Two years later, in 1878, the 2nd Battalion were posted to Rawalpindi in India, but the Buckley family did not sail to the Subcontinent with John's comrades. By now the family were billeted in what is now the Greater Manchester area. In 1881 the Cardwell Army reforms had linked regiments to different counties and cities in Britain. The 8th of Foot became the King's Liverpool Regiment and had increasingly strong links with the east Manchester area. Although no longer serving with his regiment abroad, John Buckley was still a regular soldier for another couple of years. During this time he was involved in establishing the training of part-time volunteer soldiers. He finally left the mainstream Army in April 1880 just a few days short of twenty-one years' service. However, John Buckley maintained his links with the Army when he was placed 'on reserve' with the 6th Royal Lancashire Militia in Salford. This was the usual practice for a demobbed man and required him to be involved in military training for two weeks each year. He could also be called back to the 'Colours' if the Government needed to increase the size of the Army in times of international crisis.

Upon leaving the Army John Buckley took over a public house called The Founders' Arms in Salford. He made a good income from brewing and selling ale to soldiers at barracks in the area as his family continued to grow. Six more children were born in places around Urmston such as Ashton-under-Lyne and Salford. By the standards of the late Victorian period a family of this size was quite common.

Within a couple of years John Buckley had left the licence trade and had returned to the Army on a part-time basis. Frank Buckley's birth certificate describes John as a 'Sergeant Instructor of Volunteers' and the census returns of 1891 list his occupation as 'Military Instructor'. By now the family was well established among the civilian population of Urmston. At the age of forty-nine, John Buckley would have been happy working in a field he knew very well. His hard-earned military skills had not been allowed to go to waste and as an 'old sweat' he was responsible for the military training of the part-time local yeomanry and territorial units that represented Britain's Army reserve at the time. He was actually attached to the Manchester Regiment Volunteer Battalion, which had various bases throughout the Manchester area, including Flixton, the district neighbouring Urmston.

Frank's older brothers Benjamin, Edward and Matthew played football for local amateur clubs at weekends. These clubs included the Manchester Ship Canal Football Club. They were employed during the week as 'warehousemen'.

Unlike their younger siblings, the older Buckley boys did not eventually become professional footballers. The eldest brother, Benjamin, started his working life as a warehouseman, but eventually became a professional musician. He played the French horn to a very high standard and at times even appeared among the ranks of the world-famous Hallé Orchestra. Another brother, Edward (sometimes called by his middle name, Alfred) became a salesman for the Halifax Building Society. His son entered the Roman Catholic priesthood and eventually undertook clerical and pastoral duties in the Blackpool area. Matthew Buckley was to remain in the Urmston area, becoming an upholsterer and wallpaper shop owner in Davyhulme. Frank's older sister Emily went into 'service' and became a children's governess. In 1906 she married an American called Oscar Angel. Angel acted as company secretary to a firm involving members of the Buckley family that was formed in 1908. 'Buckley & Buckley The Floorlayers Limited' was a firm that specialised in supplying and laying linoleum to premises in the Blackpool and Lytham St Annes area of western Lancashire. The major shareholder was Margaret Buckley, although Frank's brothers Benjamin and Christopher also held shares. In 1913, after the company had effectively ceased trading, Oscar and Emily emigrated to the United States, where they did very well. Oscar became a successful features writer and gained fame in the 1950s as a scriptwriter for the Warner Brothers' popular Western television series *Rawhide*. As their social status grew, Emily insisted on being called by the more sophisticated name of 'Amelia'. Despite the huge distance between them, Frank and his sister always remained in touch. His American nephews and nieces kept newspaper cuttings detailing his exploits and fame as a football player and later club manager.

Frank Buckley wrote little of his childhood or his family, but did state that he played a lot of football as a lad. He is quoted as saying, 'As a boy I played with players much my senior. I was sought by many junior clubs in that great city [Manchester].'

The family would have been described as 'respectable working class', as were their neighbours. Although close to the cotton manufacturing centre of Manchester, many of the people in Urmston were employed in places other than the mills. A good many worked for the railways and the fact that several gave their occupation as 'agricultural workers' indicates that Urmston still had rural facets to its character and was not as built up as were the central areas of local cities. This harked back to the time when Urmston was a village in its own right, but with increasing urbanisation it was becoming more and more a suburb of Manchester. Nonetheless, during the 1890s Urmston could also boast several residents described as 'managers' and 'traders'. It was home to families from as far afield as Switzerland! So all in all there was a good mixture of social classes and nationalities in the Urmston of Frank Buckley's childhood. However, the family experienced some problems when it came to religion. Like other areas of Britain, Urmston had experienced a large influx of migrants seeking work in factories and mines throughout the nineteenth century. Despite an increase in Roman Catholicism in Lancashire at the time (due mainly to Irish immigrants) the Buckley family experienced some difficulties in practising their faith. Local Catholics had met for worship in a small school as Urmston started to grow in the 1880s. It wasn't until 1889 that a plot of land was bought in Roseneath Road by a Monsignor Kershaw upon which a 'small iron church, paid for by Lady Trafford' was erected in 1893. Athough a parish church was established where the family might hear Mass, there was no school in the area where Frank and other younger male members of the family might receive a Catholic education. However, such an institution existed twenty–five miles away in Liverpool. This was St Francis Xavier's College.

St Francis Xavier College, Liverpool, in the late nineteenth century.

Urmston railway station, 1896.

Early each weekday morning during term time Franklin would walk the short distance from the family home at 19 Newton Street in Urmston to the village railway station, where he would catch a 'workingman's train' to Lime Street in Liverpool. Lasting less than an hour, Frank's daily train journey along the first passenger line in the world would have cost about 3*d* each way (equivalent to just over a modern penny). This was cheap because in order to encourage working-class commuters the government of the time had legislated that private railway companies had to put on at least one return train on each of their lines that would cost passengers no more than 1*d* for each mile they travelled. As a child traveller Frank paid a great deal less. After arriving at the terminus, Frank, dressed in a school uniform of an Eton jacket and knickerbockers and carrying his books and sandwiches, had to walk the quarter-mile through the crowded Liverpool streets from Lime Street to the College in Salisbury Street.

The Society of Jesus had founded St Francis Xavier's College for Boys in Liverpool in 1842. The Jesuits in their black robes were well known for their dedication to giving firm and unequivocal instruction to their pupils. They had founded the college in Salisbury Street to give Catholic teaching to boys of the area. The majority of the all-male teaching staff were Irish and renowned for strict discipline. The fees charged by the school (about £8 per quarter) may well have been beyond the reach of the Buckley family. It is likely that Frank Buckley would have gained admission to St Francis' by passing an entrance examination in the late spring of 1893. The college had about 275 pupils in the 'Upper School' (ten-to-sixteen-year-olds) at that time. The majority came from a lower-middle-class social background (retailers, clerks etc.). Buckley would have been one of the thirty per cent or so of pupils who came from outside the city of Liverpool. Upon entering the college as a 'Scholar' in the September of that year, Frank Buckley found the discipline strict but enjoyed the sports and physical activities that were an integral part of the Jesuit philosophy of 'muscular Christianity'. Developing into a strapping youth who enjoyed all sporting activities, Frank stayed on at school a year longer than most youngsters did at the time. He left the school in 1898 at the age of fifteen. Frank's younger brother Christopher (born in 1886) went to a newly opened Catholic school in Victoria Park in Manchester. This was run by the Xaverian Brothers but was only established after Frank had gone to grammar school.

Putting his grammar school education to good use, Frank took a job as an office clerk. Compared to other members of his family this represented quite a rise in social status. However, he spent his weekends and at least one evening a week with the Army reserve unit of which his father was the full-time physical instructor Sergeant. Frank enjoyed the active life and the camaraderie of being a 'Saturday night soldier' with the 1st Volunteer Battalion of the Manchester Regiment to such an extent that he enlisted in the Army as a full-time regular soldier. On 24 February 1900 he signed up in Manchester for a twelve-year engagement with his father's old outfit, the 2nd Battalion of the King's Liverpool Regiment. Frank was duly sent off to join his new regiment the following day. On the enlistment papers, which he signed in front of a magistrate, Buckley claimed to be over eighteen years of age. He was in fact a full year younger. However, by lying about his age, he would be accepted as a 'Regular' rather than a 'Boy' soldier, and thus receive a higher scale of pay as well as having a greater chance of serving overseas.

Originally called the '8th of Foot', this regiment was renamed the King's Liverpool Regiment during one of the Army's reorganisations in the middle of the nineteenth century when units were given a regional location with which to identify. Signing on for twelve years (seven of which were to be on active service, five on 'reserve'), Frank Buckley joined the 2nd Battalion of the King's with a view to serving in South Africa. A few months prior to this, Britain had started fighting what was to become a protracted and bloody war against Dutch settlers known as 'Boers'. There was great excitement and anger in the country at the time, resulting in many like Frank Buckley 'taking the Queen's shilling' and joining up. The towns of Kimberley and Ladysmith were being besieged by irregular Boer troops and only a month before Britain had suffered the humiliation of 1,500 men killed or captured at a place called Spion Kop.

Despite his desire to see action, Frank was not posted to South Africa or indeed any of the other colonies of the British Empire, but was sent to Ireland on what was termed a 'home posting'.

The British Government had always kept a strong military presence in Ireland to counter the strong nationalist movement there. There were fears at the time of the outbreak of the Second Boer War that Fenians and other Irish separatists would start a rebellion while British forces were on service in South Africa. Buckley's new regiment, along with others, was charged with 'keeping the peace'. For the next five years they were posted to various towns and cities in Ireland, including Belfast, Enniskillen, the Curragh and Limerick. Although Buckley himself did not go to fight against the Boers, many of his fellows did as the 2nd Battalion was used as a manpower reserve for its sister battalion, the 1st. This Battalion of the King's Liverpool Regiment had themselves suffered heavy losses at the Battle of Spion Kop – a name still remembered by Liverpudlians in the famous 'Kop End' at Anfield.

There was great concern at the time about the educational and physical fitness levels among young men volunteering for the British Armed Forces. Many saw the Army as a way to escape the deprivations of the industrial towns and cities of Britain and travel to exotic places throughout the Empire by joining up. However, despite their enthusiasm to join the Colours, the effects of poor diet and the unsanitary living conditions many had suffered made the rejection rate of applicants high. This, coupled with the number of recruits unable to read or calculate at any but the most basic level, led to public concern evident even within government circles. The level of national anxiety can be gauged from the nature and intensity of subsequent legislation on public health and education reform.

So it can be seen why a willing recruit with Frank Buckley's educational background and physical prowess was welcomed with open arms. Upon entering the Army Frank Buckley measured 5ft 9in in height but weighed a mere 10st 5lbs. However, he was to gain weight and grow to nearly 6ft tall while serving in the Army.

Although Frank Buckley did not see active service while with the King's, it does not mean he had an easy life. Like other recruits he was issued with two sets of clothing, which for many from poor backgrounds may have seemed a rare luxury. However, often these uniforms were ill fitting and the new man had to pay the regimental tailor to alter them to fit. It was well known to more experienced soldiers that a swindle often took place during this process. The tailor (aptly described as the 'official alterer of ill-fitting off-the-peg uniforms'), having made chalk marks on the uniforms in line with the man's measurements, then took the uniforms away, rubbed out the marks and returned the uniforms untouched!

Recruits suffered other forms of low-level racketeering by older hands. Accounts from other young soldiers serving in Ireland at the time noted that

> The corporal to whom the recruits had handed their civilian clothes
> for safe keeping, sold the lot to a dealer and denied that he had ever set
> eyes on them. Two old soldiers, put in to share the barrack room with

14 recruits and to give big-brotherly help and advice, were sparing with the help but were active in monopolising the best of the food. They also enforced a compulsory weekly cash levy on each man for the hire of cleaning kit (even though everyone already had their own). The men also had to pay NCOs for the completion of weekend leave passes which merely meant the filling in of the man's name and the date. The recruits were also swindled when it came to having their uniforms cleaned. Soldiers' wives, like the tailor, were paid from public funds to do the recruits' laundry. They dumped it all in one tub of water, wrung it out, dried it, and gave it back. It stank.

Buckley's day would be well orchestrated and disciplined and would be along the following lines. At 5 a.m. he would be awoken by the company bugler blasting out the shrill notes of 'Reveille'. He would then have to make his bed, help tidy the barrack room and prepare for the first parade of the day at a quarter to six. Following this, an hour would be taken up with physical exercise and rifle drill, which concluded with an extended run around the parade ground. Breakfast, usually consisting of bread and butter washed down with strong tea, was served at 7 a.m. As a special treat, jam and even the odd rasher of bacon were available for breakfast on special occasions. Then the barrack room had to be thoroughly cleaned and tables scrubbed for a 9 a.m. accommodation and kit inspection. Any failure to meet the required standard by an individual could result in the Sergeant-Major imposing extra duties on the whole of the barrack hut as a punishment, so the men soon learnt to look out for each other. Marching and parade drill took up the next ninety minutes or so. This was followed by an equal amount of time given over to gymnastics. This was 'a hard grind; 14 presses between the parallel bars, 14 pulls to the chest on the horizontal bar, climbing the walls by fingertip and toe grips, walking along a plank in the rafters, jumping to catch a rope hanging from the ceiling and going down it hand over hand to the floor again'. At midday dinner was served to the soldiers who would have been very hungry indeed after a morning of relentless physical activity. The meal would consist of the very stodgy fare of meat, potatoes, vegetables and a pudding described as 'seldom appetising', and was filling rather than nourishing. However, it was considered adequate to sustain a further one-hour's drill in full marching order. The men had tea at 4.30 p.m. and this was the final meal of the day. If their regulation daily ration of 1lb of bread had been consumed at breakfast the tired recruit only had tea to drink and had nothing more to eat until the next morning.

One might imagine that the boring unimaginative monotony of his daily routine, with its repetition of barrack square drill, gymnastics, equipment and barrack room cleaning, might have deterred Frank Buckley, but it seems the opposite was true. Buckley coped well with this routine and gradually made his way through the ranks. Within five months of enlisting he wrote that he had been promoted to the rank of Lance-Corporal and was made up to full Corporal by September 1900. He became an unpaid Lance Sergeant in September 1902 and finally Buckley's physical skills and hard work eventually gained him the rank of Gymnastics Instructor (First Class) in January 1903. He had successfully passed a certificate course at the Army's base at Aldershot. Frank Buckley also successfully acquired the Army's Certificates of Education in 1900, although these dealt only with basic abilities and achievements (such as the ability to read simple sentences). They did not prove difficult to someone with Frank's educational background.

During his five years in Ireland, Frank Buckley's love of sport grew. He represented his regiment at rugby, cricket and, of course, football. His football skills and ability were such that he received a letter from his commanding officer, Lieutenant Charles Harrington, complimenting him on his

footballing talent. Frank Buckley was very proud of this rec-
ognition and remarked on his respect for Harrington, who
refused to take a field commission promotion during the
fighting at Orange River in South Africa. However he was
awarded the DSO in 1900 and eventually became Deputy
Chief of the Imperial General Staff in 1918. Harrington was
knighted in 1919.

Buckley loved his football and often saw the funny side
of the sport. He recounted a tale of the time he was playing in Ireland in an inter-company match. The goalkeeper
of Buckley's team (whom he described as 'one of those
excitable chaps who would swear that black was white')
had to defend a goal that did not have the luxury of a net.
Playing against them was a Quartermaster-Sergeant named
Jones, who had been on the books of Aston Villa. Jones
duly scored a fine goal, but as there were no nets Buckley's
'keeper declared that the ball had gone outside the post and
a goal had not been scored. A melee ensued and in a fit of
pique the goalkeeper picked up the ball and ran off. As the
game could not continue without the ball, the 'keeper was
subsequently put under military arrest and was marched off
to the guardroom – a very different approach to handling
dissent compared with today!

Buckley always said it was the Army that was responsible
for him becoming a professional player. In the spring of 1903
the King's Liverpool Regiment football team met that of
the Lancashire Fusiliers in the final of the Irish Cup. The
game was played at Dalymount Park in Dublin. Although
on the side defeated by the only goal, Buckley was 'spotted'
by an Aston Villa scout who suggested he go to England
for a trial. After a successful trial against Ironbridge Town,
from Shropshire, the Villa offered Buckley an 'engagement',
which he accepted. Although he later wrote that he had
been 'lured by the seductive voice' of George Ramsay, the
Villa club secretary, who had convinced Buckley he was

'a heaven sent exponent of football', there is no doubt that Frank Buckley was ready for a new challenge by following the path of the sport in which he had talent and ability – football.

On 30 April 1903, Frank Buckley paid the then-huge fee of £18 and 'bought himself out' of the Army. He was given the money to do this by a widow he was courting at the time. Her name was Martha Robinson, although everyone called her Madge. She would eventually become Frank's wife. Although he had completed only three years and sixty-six days of his planned five years' active service, he had not seen the last of the Army, although further involvement was some ten years into the future.

Together with his younger brother Chris (also a footballer) he moved near to the small town of Redditch, to the south of Birmingham, where they were employed as part-time pig farmers on Lodge Farm in the village of Ipsley. However, to Frank this job was of secondary importance because by this time his professional football career had started.

TWO

THE WANDERING MINSTREL

Frank Buckley called the years between leaving the Army in 1903 and re-enlisting at the outbreak of the First World War in 1914 the time of being 'a wandering minstrel'. He was of course referring to the number of football clubs for which he played during this period – eight in all, including signing for the Villa twice.

The decade during which Buckley was to play his professional football was a period not only of consolidation but of steady growth for the sport. Football had evolved during the latter part of the nineteenth century. It was originally a pastime of the upper and middle social classes, with matches often taking place at public schools or on regimental playing fields; it became the major sport of the working classes of the industrial centres of Britain. While cricket and to some extent rugby had been able to maintain the established social status of 'Gentlemen' and 'Players', the advent of full-time paid players in football had led to accusations that it was the 'sport of the greedy'. Nonetheless its popularity grew. Even though there remained a peppering of 'gentle-man-amateurs' in football clubs prior to 1912, they became an increasingly rare breed and an echo of former days.

The advent of the Football League in 1888 and the organisational structure of cup competitions, leagues and divisions gave increasingly affluent industrial workers the means of enjoying a social activity on a Saturday after-noon. It also gave them the means of loyally identifying with their town or locality. It was at this time that most of the present locally based professional clubs were formed in Britain. The huge expansion of football in the quarter of a century before the First World War was accompanied by a comparative growth in related economic activity. Transfer fees between clubs became commonplace, but the direc-tors of clubs, men who owned what were in fact limited companies, kept most of the profit on such dealings. In this respect, football clubs reflected the structure of many of Britain's industrial and commercial concerns. Whether in pursuit of profit or the avoidance of bankruptcy, sharp practice and deceit – evident in the less salubrious areas of commercial life – were to be found in football at this time. Bribery and the 'fixing' of matches was fairly widespread and a constant source of worry to the Football Association. Unscrupulous club directors would cut many corners to maximise their own gains and this was extremely detrimen-tal to the sport. During his playing career, Frank Buckley became very aware of the situation that could exist within a club's management structure. He learned not to place all his trust in the directors of a club he was associated with. This attitude was to stay with him right through his career as a manager. Years later Buckley said he 'believed all clubs should have one director – and he should be dead!'

However, after leaving the Army, Buckley's first profes-sional signing was for Aston Villa, whom he called, 'the most outstanding club at that time'. He was not the only former soldier in Villa's ranks. A player named Crabtree had also been bought out of the Army to join the club, and alongside him were other famous players of the time, including Wilkes, Spencer and Franks. Harry Hampton, the famous centre forward, was signed by the Midlands club on the same day that Franklin Buckley put pen to paper.

Frank was filled with great hopes that he would quickly become an established player in the first XI and that his new career would progress rapidly. Interestingly, he played his first professional game against Wolves, the club he would become famous for managing. By this time he had established that his best position was that of a robust half-back – a position that has been accurately likened to that of a modern-day attacking centre half. Despite the skills and stamina he had built up while in the Army, Buckley found the transition to civilian football very difficult. He said that he was an 'utter novice at the game' compared with others at Villa. An improvement in his play was brought about by 'perseverance and hard work, together with the advice of older and more experienced players'. Nonetheless, despite holding a regular place in Villa's reserve team, Buckley felt the chance of promotion to the first XI was remote. In 1905 he left Villa and, along with his brother Chris, joined Brighton Football Club. At the time there was no national football organisational structure in the way there is today. Despite the existence of the Football League, a rival organisation was to be found in the 'Southern League'. This latter body was entirely self-controlled and administered, and only accountable to the Football Association for its actions. There was no working agreement between the two leagues on transfer issues, so the Buckley brothers were able to join Brighton without transfer fees being paid to Villa. Chris Buckley later renewed his association with Aston Villa and eventually became chairman of the board of directors in the inter-war period.

It was while on the books of Brighton that Franklin Buckley married for the first time. On 4 October 1905 Frank married Martha (better known as Madge) Robinson at the Chorlton registry office in his home city of Manchester. Franklin was twenty-two years of age and his new bride was over twelve years older than he was. Madge (whose maiden name was Daniels) was the daughter of a pattern-maker and had been born in Staffordshire. She had moved with her husband George to Manchester in the 1890s where he had become a successful cotton handkerchief manufacturer. However, she had been widowed in her late twenties and had met Buckley while living near to his family when he was younger. Madge had been left well off when she was widowed, and there is no doubt she was very much in love with her new young and handsome husband. Madge bore Frank a son, whom they christened Jack. However, the marriage of Frank and Madge was very nearly a short-lived affair. Soon after the wedding a domestic catastrophe occurred that almost brought about the end of Frank Buckley's playing career and indeed the lives of himself and his new wife. During the First World War a newspaper article told of Frank Buckley being involved in a very serious house fire in the period after he had left the King's Regiment. It seems that he and Madge had moved to the Solihull area with the intention of rearing cattle and horses. This venture was an extension of the pig-breeding business that Frank Buckley and his brother Chris had become involved in a few years earlier, which had been financed by Madge. It provided the brothers with good incomes, and thus allowed them not to become reliant on wages from any football team they played for. Although the article states that Buckley and his wife were living at 'Monkspath Priory' near Solihull, this Victorian house had been derelict for some time. However, records of a serious house fire occurring in the area in 1905 do exist. An account of a fire in a large

*Madge Buckley in
1924. (Mrs M. Powell
and family collection)*

property called the 'Hermitage' in Lode Lane, Solihull, tells
how the 'Lady of the House' only managed to get out just
before the upper floors of the building collapsed. The family
moved to a house in Yardley Wood, which was closer to
Birmingham, but continued to breed farm animals. The
article concludes by saying that Frank Buckley had become
a 'gentleman farmer' and that his wife ('a business woman in
her own right') bred 'prize–winning cattle and horses'. They
had certainly come a long way from the humble streets of
Manchester.

Frank's close relationship to his brother Chris was inten-
sified in late 1910, when Chris married Madge's daughter
Mignon in Ipsley. Effectively, Frank Buckley became his
brother's stepfather-in-law, and when Chris and Mignon
had children he was both their uncle and grandfather at
the same time!

After just one season playing for Brighton, Frank Buckley was still dissatisfied and sought another change of team. He returned north to his native Manchester and signed for United. At that time Manchester United played at a ground called Bank Lane and Buckley recalled an incident on the pitch that he called 'one of the most harrowing of his life'. During a local reserve derby match against St Helens Town, Blackstock (one of the United full-backs) staggered and fell after passing the ball to Buckley. The game was immediately halted and Frank helped in carrying Blackstock to the changing room. Much to everyone's horror they found that the player was dead! It appears he died of a heart attack or seizure, but the incident became an enduring memory that stayed with Frank Buckley for many years.

Although he made only 3 first-team appearances, the season Buckley played for United was a good one. This was not only because they beat his former club, the mighty Villa, in the FA Cup, but also because after twelve unhappy seasons in the Second Division, 1906 was the year that United finally claimed their place again in the top flight. At the time United had an outstanding manager called Ernest Mangnall. Ever boasting of their Johnny-come-lately club's influence and achievements, one historian of United has even claimed, 'no doubt some of Mangnall's wisdom rubbed off on the young man [Buckley]'. There is no evidence for this as Buckley was to become innovative and unique in his approach to football management. He was always ready to acknowledge the role models of his past, yet nowhere does he mention Mangnall.

However, even being on the books of such a successful club could not persuade him to stay put. After only staying for one season with United, Frank's lack of first-team games gave him wanderlust in his football boots and he was on the move again. He signed again for the Villa for just a few weeks at the end of the 1906/07 season, but after once more failing to be selected for any first-team matches, he soon headed north again. Arriving back again in his hometown he headed for the blue side of Manchester and signed for City at the start of the 1907/08 season.

At the start of the season when Buckley had been with United a major scandal had erupted concerning their neighbours Manchester City. It seems that players were all supposed to be on a fixed wage of £4 per game but it was discovered that City had been paying £6 or £7 a week to each player. The FA was furious about this discovery and dismissed five of the Manchester City directors. They also forbade seventeen of the club's players from ever appearing in a blue shirt again. United took advantage of their neighbours' plight and signed several City players, including the famous Billy Meredith (popularly known as the 'Welsh Wizard'). Described as the 'George Best of the Edwardian era – rebellious, skilled and popular', Meredith was also said to have been involved in bribery and corruption to the point where it was claimed he was lucky not to be banned from the game for life. Interestingly, because the City players signed by United in 1906 were all serving FA-mandated suspensions, they did not make their debuts for the Reds until 1907. Even though he worked with these players at United, there is no evidence or suggestion that Frank Buckley was tainted by their practices. Rather more to the point is that, being aware of this darker side of the sport, Buckley always declared that he wanted matters to be up front and in the open. He retained this approach throughout the remainder of his playing days and on into his career as a manager.

After a couple of uneventful seasons among the depleted ranks of Manchester City, Frank Buckley moved back to the Midlands and joined Birmingham City in 1909. Being able to travel easily to St Andrew's from his south Birmingham home, he enjoyed regular first-team football with the Blues, although they did not experience very much success. At the end of his first season with Birmingham, the club found themselves at the bottom of the two divisions that made up the Football League at that time. Birmingham City were fortunate enough to be re-elected straight back into the League. The following season a former Blues player called Bob Roberts was appointed manager and their league position improved. This was significant because prior to this the usual procedure had been for the directors of a football club to appoint players into a club's squad, while club secretaries would decide on tactics and team selection each week. Roberts had far more influence on all aspects of the club and drew together the roles of the directors and the secretary in on-field activity. He recommended which players the club should purchase on the transfer market and he decided on team selection and the tactics to be used in each game. None of this would have been lost on Frank Buckley and may well have influenced his own approach to football management in later years. In all, Frank Buckley played 56 games and scored several goals for Birmingham City in the two seasons up to August 1911.

The following autumn saw Frank Buckley arrive at the penultimate club of his playing career, Derby County, and it was at Derby where he was to reach his greatest achievements as a player. Derby County had had a bit of a rollercoaster history, but Frank Buckley joined them and played during a very successful season. He described them as 'a grand side'. When he came from Birmingham, he joined the heart of Derby's defence alongside Charlie Betts (another new signing, from Newcastle). Strangely, there were five other regular members of the Derby side whose surnames began with the letter 'B'. It was no surprise that the team became nicknamed 'the Busy Bees'. Most famous of the Derby 'B's was the legendary Steve Bloomer.

Bloomer had been born in the Black Country town of Cradley Heath in 1874 and had gained prominence with Derby County between 1891 and 1906. Although he played for Middlesbrough between 1906 and 1910, he returned to Derby in time for the 1911/12 season. As captain, he was instrumental in inspiring the team to win the Second Division championship in 1912. He recognised Buckley's part in this success and always stated that Frank Buckley should have captained the side that season. For his part, Buckley wrote that Steve Bloomer was the 'greatest inside forward of all time' and always considered that he had been very privileged to have been in the same team as him. Bloomer is often considered unfortunate to have been coaching in Berlin at the outbreak of the First World War. He was interned by the Germans when hostilities broke out but, considering the loss of life among footballers who joined up on both sides, Bloomer's captivity in Germany may well have saved his life.

Buckley's defensive performances for Derby during their promotion season of 1911 and the subsequent two seasons brought him to the attention of the England selectors. Much to his honour and delight, at the age of thirty-one he was chosen to play for England against the Irish in a Home Championship match in February 1914.

The match took place at Middlesbrough Football Club, with England expected to trounce the lowly Irish side. Frank Buckley lined up with other well-known internationals of the time, including Jesse Pennington of West Bromwich Albion, who was undoubtedly England's most famous pre-war player. Buckley cut a fine figure, being described in the press at the time as 'tall, heavily built, pivotal, hard working and forceful when attacking'. A few eyebrows were raised when the score remained goal-less at half-time and most spectators, and indeed the country at large, were shocked when the Irish emerged as eventual 3-0 winners. The

London Times declared that the Irish were worthy winners on the day. The English defenders, Pennington and Cuggy of Sunderland, were well beaten by the Irish forwards, Lacey and Gillespie. Frank Buckley was not found culpable for any of the goals.

'Ever restless', Buckley moved from Derby to Bradford City. Although he did not know it at the time, his playing career was all but over. The 4 occasions that he turned out for the Bantams in the hot late summer of 1914 were to be the final games of his career. He was never again picked to play for England. Indeed there was only one further international football game on English soil that year because of serious international events taking place. The assassination of an obscure member of the Austro-Hungarian royal family in the far-off Balkans meant Frank Buckley was to become involved in a far bigger international match – the First World War!

THREE

THE GREAT
INTERNATIONAL

There were many reasons for the outbreak of the First
World War in Europe in the summer of 1914, but few
people at the time could have realised the enormous effect
this war would have. The consequences of the struggle
between the Great Powers would not only affect empires,
states and national economies, but would also shape the
destinies of ordinary people – people like Frank Buckley.

Britain had always tried to remain in 'splendid isolation'
from events in Europe. However, staying neutral in the
conflict between the continental Great Powers was not an
option after the beginning of August that year. As part of
her strategy to defeat the French, Germany indicated her
intention of invading neutral Belgium. As a guarantor of
Belgium's independence, Britain declared war on Germany,
and her involvement in the First World War was secured.

Being an island state and having a huge overseas empire,
Britain's military policy had been focused mainly on maintaining a strong navy and a relatively small army for many

years. The regular Army and reservists were all volunteers and were few in number compared with the conscripted armies of the Continent. The British Army comprised only 450,000 men, including only around 900 trained staff officers and some 250,000 reservists. Although well trained, they were poorly equipped and armed. Nonetheless, they gave a very good account of themselves in the early clashes with the Germans in the late summer of 1914. It was this expeditionary force that had held up the German advance at the town of Mons, thus giving the French Army time to regroup around Paris. The German Kaiser showed his nation's frustration at being so thwarted by bitterly referring to the British as 'a contempt-ible little army'. Veterans of this force were always proud to call themselves 'Old Contemptibles', but the Battle of Mons and the subsequent retreat towards Paris took a heavy toll on their numbers. In fact, the first three months of fighting cost the British Expeditionary Force some 50,000 casualties, of which the bulk was infantry. By 1 November, of the eighty-four battalions Britain had sent onto the Continent, only nine had over 300 fit men and eighteen had less than 100. It was quickly realised in London that more men would be needed if defeat were to be avoided.

Being used to short colonial wars, many in high office fully expected the war to be 'over by Christmas', although Lord Kitchener, the newly appointed Secretary for War, took a more realistic view. He warned that the outcome of the war would be decided by the last million men Britain could throw into the fray. It has been estimated that the Army needed 600 new recruits per day to replace the casualties from the BEF. As enforced conscription was seen as being against the indi-vidual Briton's freedoms, he decided on raising a new army of volunteers. Two days after war had been declared, Parliament gave permission for the Army to be increased to a strength of 500,000 men. A few days later on 7 August, Lord Kitchener made his first appeal for 100,000 volunteers. Recruits had to be single, aged between nineteen and thirty, at least 5ft 3ins tall and with a chest size greater than 34ins. This was officially called the 'First New Army' but was more popularly known as 'K1'. Married men were later allowed to enlist and further waves of recruits were designated 'K2', 'K3', up to 'K5'. The appeal for new troops was aided by a suggestion from General Henry Rawlinson that men would be more willing to join up if they could serve with people they already knew. Peer pressure and the influence of friends would encourage those uncertain of joining up. This approach was very successful, as was shown by Lord Derby. He made public in late August 1914 that he would try and raise a 'Battalion of Pals' from among the men of Liverpool. In less than a week he had enough men to make up four battalions!

Filled with patriotic fervour, men began to stream into the Forces to such an extent that weapon and uniform manufacture could not keep up with the numbers joining. Many new recruits took part in drills and training during the daytime but were sent home at night because of the scarcity of Army billets. The call to arms was strong throughout the land and all fit men were expected to go!

Against this background, professional footballers like Frank Buckley had encountered a great problem. Cricket and rugby competitions ceased almost immediately war was declared, allowing team members to join up. Footballers, however, were tied to clubs through one-year renewable contracts. In effect it meant that, whether they wished to enlist or not, professional players were legally unable to do so as they could be prosecuted by their clubs for breaking their contracts. The football clubs were, after all, businesses, and in light of the current feeling that the war would be a short one, saw no urgency in releasing their players from legally binding contracts. It was also argued at the time that no other business was expected to effectively close down voluntarily, so why should football be singled out?

The general public did not see matters in the same way, and in the red mist of 'War Fever' professional players were accused of cowardice and shirking their patriotic duty. Matchday attendances dropped sharply and players were vilified publicly. It was even reported that Manchester United players were spat at in the street, popular public feelings were running so high. Clergy preached from the pulpit that enlistment by footballers was in the 'right spirit'. Players were advised to 'Go straight to the recruiting officer and offer yourself. This is the plain duty of every able-bodied young man today.' Even the world famous creator of Sherlock Holmes, Sir Arthur Conan Doyle, appealed for footballers to rally to the Colours in a recruiting speech he delivered on 6 September 1914:

> There was a time for all things in the world. There was a time for games, there was a time for business, and there was a time for domestic life. There was a time for everything, but there is only time for one thing now, and that thing is war. If the cricketer had a straight eye let him look along the barrel of a rifle. If a footballer had strength of limb let them serve and march in the field of battle.

The whole matter of footballers joining up became a national *cause celebre* and a fierce debate as to the morality of clubs continuing to play raged in the national press. The strength of feeling was very high and clubs were even accused of being traitors to Britain! As A.F. Pollard wrote in *The Times*:

> We view with indignation and alarm the persistence of Association Football Clubs in doing their best for the enemy. There is no excuse from diverting from the Front thousands of athletes in order to feast the eyes of crowds of inactive spectators who are unfit to fight or else unfit to be fought for.

A more conciliatory note was sounded a few days later on 14 October, when William Beckett wrote to *The Times*. He suggested establishing regional bases (e.g. in London and the North-West) where footballers could train when not appearing for their clubs. He went on to suggest that a 'professional football brigade could be formed', and because training would take a long time, they might complete the current football season. In this way footballers 'would be proud to keep the flag flying and the ball rolling at the same time'.

The FA bowed to pressure somewhat by appealing to single men to join up and, in conjunction with the War Office, organised recruiting drives at matches. This was a complete disaster as only one recruit came forward at Arsenal's game and none at all when Nottingham Forest played. The press mocked the FA's efforts, although the association hit back stating that the game had produced 100,000 recruits in four months and only 600 single men who made a living from the game had not offered to enlist, compared with 2 million other potential recruits who were still not in the Services. This cut no ice, and pressure on the association continued. Attendances continued to fall and the government imposed an entertainment tax on clubs, forcing them to cut players' wages. While professional football continued, clubs were forced to pay twenty per cent of all gate receipts to a general pool for government use. They also had to donate four per cent of takings to charity and pay a further one per cent to the League.

The pressure on the FA to suspend leagues and competitions increased even more in late autumn 1914 when Mrs Cunliffe-Owen got permission from Lord Kitchener to raise a 'Sportsman's Battalion'. Although not a locally based 'Pals' unit, members of this battalion shared a common interest and were seen in the same way as the 'Pals'. The battalion contained famous cricketers and boxers, but notably no footballers!

The situation could not continue. At a meeting held in London in December 1914 the issue was resolved. Present at the meeting was a representative of the Football Association named Fredrick Wall and a wealthy MP, William Joyson-Hicks. It was decided to form a battalion of footballers, which would be part of the Middlesex Regiment. This battalion was to be part of 'K3', (the third 'New Army').

William Joyson-Hicks, commonly known as 'Jix', was born in 1865 in Canonbury and came from a very humble background. Originally, his surname was just Hicks, but he married into a wealthy Manchester silk manufacturing family called Joyson in the 1890s and adopted his in-laws' surname. A lifelong Conservative, he took a great interest in the formation of the Royal Flying Corps (forerunner to the RAF) as well as the Footballers' Battalion. He eventually became Home Secretary during the 1926 General Strike and was made Viscount Brentford in 1929. Joyson-Hicks died in June 1932.

Known as the 'Die-hards', the Middlesex Regiment already had one themed battalion based on the lines of the 'Pals'. This was a battalion made up of former public schoolboys, and later two battalions of local council employees known as 'public workers' were admitted into the regiment. Eventually the Middlesex Regiment was to comprise over thirty battalions, three of which were made up of footballers.

The battalion formed by Wall and Joyson-Hicks was designated the '17th Service Battalion (1st Footballers)'. It was called a 'service' battalion as it was being raised specifically for the duration of the conflict and to discern it from the regular and reserve battalions in the Middlesex Regiment.

As the regular Army had been unable to cope with the huge influx of men, they had no experienced officers or senior NCOs to spare for the service battalions. It became commonplace in the early days of the war for a retired regular officer to be appointed as commanding officer of the new unit, with perhaps one or two other experienced officers. Sometimes these officers were on leave from India or veterans of the Boer War. Other ranks of authority such as the quartermaster and the Sergeant Major would be drawn from time-served regulars. The remainder of the officers and senior NCOs were appointed from among those with any form of military experience.

The first CO of the 17th Service Battalion was Henry Thomas Fenwick. Fenwick was a fifty-one-year-old career soldier who had come from a North-Eastern brewing family. He had for a short time been a Liberal MP and was a political contemporary of Joyson-Hicks. Fenwick had been awarded the Distinguished Service Order for his bravery during the Boer War. In 1901, as Colonel of the Army's premier regiment, the Life Guards, he was decorated with the Royal Victorian Order; an award only granted by the monarch personally. He retired in 1911, but was recalled to the Colours in 1914 to lead the newly formed Footballers' Battalion.

Writing almost twenty years later, Frederick Wall recalled that the very first man to volunteer for the 17th Battalion was none other than Franklin Buckley.

Buckley's previous army experience, (albeit as an NCO), along with the leadership qualities he had shown on the foot-ball field, stood him in good stead. He was initially appointed to the battalion as a Lieutenant but just after Christmas 1914 he was promoted to the rank of Captain. Eventually he would be given the rank of Major (a 'field' promotion) and retained this title for the remainder of his life (this being permissible for ranks above that of Captain). However, Buckley's eventual rank was only ever designated as 'Temporary' Major. This was because of snobbery in the regular Army, which insisted the status quo must be maintained. All promoted senior officers of the New Armies were granted only temporary commissions and disparagingly referred to as 'Temporary

Gentlemen'. Interestingly, when Buckley was made Captain, he received back half of the £18 he had paid the Army to buy himself out in 1903! This was an unexpected and very welcome windfall!

Within weeks, the 17th Battalion had its full complement of 600 men. Quite a few of them had been drawn locally to the force by a recruiting poster asking Chelsea fans if they wanted 'to become a Die-Hard?', which was the nickname of the Middlesex Regiment. Although including football-ers from all over the United Kingdom, local involvement was indeed strong with players from Clapham Orient (later Leyton Orient) forming the largest single contingent of the new battalion. The whole of the Clapham Orient first team enlisted together, three of whom were to be killed in Flanders, alongside two sons of Lord Kinnaird, the president of the Football Association. With many famous players joining the 17th Middlesex at the recruiting office in Hammersmith, George Pike, a recruit who had played for Blyth Spartans in

Left: *Major Buckley in 1915.*

Opposite page: *Major Buckley (centre) with officers and men of the first Football Battalion, 1916. (Coloursport)*

the North-East of England, said, 'The battalion roll call read like an autograph book!' Among the more famous footballers to join Fenwick and Buckley was Vivian Woodward, who had been an England international since 1903. He was the player credited with scoring Tottenham Hotspur's first League goal (against Wolves) in 1908 and had won an Olympic gold medal for football that same year. Capped 66 times by England, Woodward was appointed Lieutenant and was later wounded at the Battle of the Somme.

Another significant figure in the ranks of the new battalion was Walter Tull, who had played for both Spurs and Northampton Town. Tull was the first black outfield player to be a professional footballer in Britain. He joined the 17th Middlesex and by the end of 1915 he had been promoted to the rank of Sergeant. Towards the end of the following year and having endured the horrors of the Battle of the Somme, Tull was sent back to England suffering from trench fever. When he had recovered and returned to the Front, he was transferred to the 23rd Battalion of the Middlesex Regiment ('Second Footballers') where he was commissioned as a Second Lieutenant. This promotion was truly a landmark in British military history, as Tull had become the first black officer in the British Army. This was completely against the King's Regulations of the time that forbade a negro to be in charge of white soldiers. Perhaps those associated with a sport now so bedevilled with elements of racism were in some way showing the rest of society a way forward. Tull's men showed their respect and regard for the man to the extent that four of them risked their lives under enemy fire to reclaim his body from No Man's Land after he was killed in March 1918.

As the regular Army were under so much pressure in France, the service battalions had to be largely left to their own devices when it came to training. In preparation for the Battle of the Somme, the 17th Middlesex Battalion moved

The Middlesex Regiment footballers arrive at Holmbury Park in the spring of 1915.

from London to Joyson-Hicks' country estate at Holmbury in Surrey in the spring of 1915. Although players were still permitted to turn out for their clubs at weekends if so requested, the battalion got down to serious training (what Buckley called 'learning the lessons of war'). Early morning kit inspection, physical training and route marches were followed by trench digging and weapons training. Although hard work, this period was not without its funny side – one poor recruit was berated by Sergeant Major McFadden that he 'could not shoot as a soldier, just as he could not shoot as a footballer!' Belonging to an infantry regiment, the men of the 17th were trained in marksmanship with Lee-Enfield .303 rifles. They also undertook bayonet practice on bags of straw suspended from trees growing in the estate's parkland. Apart from the domestic chores of camp life, the men had little free time for social activity, although Buckley did manage to occasionally visit Madge, who was living on a farm in Yardley Wood near Birmingham. By the early summer of 1915, with all football competitions finally suspended and training completed, the regiment embarked for France and the hell-hole known as 'the Western Front'.

The battalion sailed for France and was assigned to the 100th Brigade of the 33rd Division. Over the course of the next three months they occupied various temporary billets near the Franco-Belgium border. However, the main role of the 17th Middlesex was to become part of a huge force the British commander, Douglas Haig, was massing in the central area of the battlefront. After the Germans had been halted and pushed some way back in 1914, a stagnant trench war had developed between the two sides. Haig planned to break the deadlock in July 1916 by breaking through the German lines at the river Somme. Buckley and the Football Battalion were to be part of the second element of the plan, and were to be used to consolidate and hold captured ground after the enemy had been forced out.

By November 1915 the footballers had established themselves in a small French town called Guarbecque. Here they
spent their time with training and the 'usual drills'. However,
on 2 December they marched the 16km to Bethume and
were billeted in a large school. Although Bethume had been
the site of some heavy fighting, the battalion's stay there was
uneventful, and even quite comfortable. This may have lulled
them into a false sense of security for what was to come. Men
were assigned training in first aid and machine gun use, each
battalion being given two such weapons for the forthcoming campaign. On 8 December they were transferred from
the 33rd Division to the 6th Brigade of the 2nd Division,
which was commanded by Brigadier General Daley. On the
afternoon of the following day they marched a short distance
to Annequin Fosse and were now actually at the battlefront.
The battalion were assigned to trenches and were put on
twenty-four-hour trench duty, which meant they were to
watch the enemy and be ready at a moment's notice to repel
any enemy attack. It was during this time that Buckley (still a
Captain) and two other officers were attached to a company
of the Royal Berkshire Regiment for a short while. As they
were new to the trenches this temporary transfer was to give
them some instruction and experience from soldiers who
were 'old hands' in trench warfare.

Over the next fortnight the footballers were involved in
skirmishes with the enemy and suffered some casualties. At
least two of their number were captured by the Germans.
As was the usual practice they were withdrawn to a rest area
after this period of trench fighting.

During the course of the next few months the footballers
were involved in very heavy fighting in the area to the east
of Arras. There are reports of them mining enemy trenches,
a process which involved digging shafts and galleries below
the German trenches and then detonating high-explosive
charges. In the words of the battalion diarist, intermittent

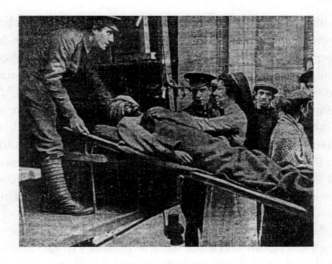

Men of the 17th Battalion Middlesex regiment helping a Sikh soldier during the Battle of the Somme, 1916.

rainstorms and enemy shelling made life 'disagreeable' – this was undoubtedly a gross understatement. The 17th Battalion was experiencing all the horrors of trench warfare: the flooding, the intermittent but heavy shelling by the enemy, the mud, the vermin and the poor food, which was often cold. There was no time for football. It was said that Leigh Roose, the Welsh international goalkeeper, employed his football throwing skills to great effect in August 1916 when hurling hand-grenades to stop a German attack. He was awarded the Military Medal for his bravery, but sadly he was killed the following October at Ligney-Tholley on the Somme.

This misery, coupled with the constant fear of being killed by a 'bullet with your name on it' affected both men and officers alike, and deep and strong bonds were formed. An incident that occurred around this time was recalled by Michael Brewer. Mr Brewer's father, Lance Sergeant Thomas Henry Brewer, and his older brother William had both played for Queens Park Rangers and had joined the 17th Middlesex Battalion together. Thomas Brewer had been given the role of Major Buckley's batman and one night he and William were ordered by the Major to stand guard and watch for activity on the enemy's side of No Man's Land. During the hours of darkness, William was shot and killed by a German sniper. The story goes that Frank Buckley was so upset that his command had resulted in the man's death that he offered to pay for the education of William Brewer's three children. Although the offer was never taken up, it shows something of the humanity behind the hard exterior that was Major Franklin Buckley.

Like all British soldiers, Frank looked forward to receiving letters from his family back in Britain. He also received pies made by his wife, which he shared with his comrades. Mrs Buckley's pies (of which it was said 'she made tons and tons') were soon a favourite among the men and a rare treat in the squalid conditions of the trenches.

When British, Canadian and other Empire troops went 'over the top' along the Somme river on the morning of 1 July 1916, it heralded the start of what Haig hoped would be the great breakthrough that would end the stalemate of the trench war. Nothing could have been further from the truth. Full of confidence that Allied artillery, which had been pounding the Germans for over a week, would have all but destroyed the enemy, many thought the initial attack would be a 'walkover'. Instead the Tommies were met by the withering machine-gun fire of German soldiers who had sheltered from the great barrage in deep, well-constructed bunkers under their trenches. By the end of the day (the 'blackest in its history') the British Army had lost over 60,000 men. The slaughter continued for the next four months, and it was said in England that there was not a family in the land that did not lose a loved one on the Somme.

In the words of Buckley himself, the 17th Battalion 'took their place' in this great battle, but they were not called upon in the initial fighting. Their division had been kept in reserve at a small town called Bryas for almost three weeks. On 20 July they were brought from Bryas by train to a reserve position at Longueau. After a week in reserve trenches on the road between Carnoy and Montauban, they were pitched into very heavy fighting at the infamous 'Delville Wood'. Along with a brigade of South Africans and men of the South Staffs Regiment, the footballers repulsed a strong enemy attack that lasted for the two days of 27 and 28 July. In the heavy fighting the regiment suffered 237 casualties, among whom was Colonel Fenwick. But far more life-threatening than Fenwick's injuries were those suffered by Frank Buckley.

A German hand grenade had landed near Buckley and had exploded. The sharp metal shrapnel had hit him in the chest and had punctured his lungs. George Pyke witnessed the incident. Unconscious and bleeding profusely, Frank Buckley was nearer to death than life and the fact that he was able to receive any medical help was almost by chance. Mr Pyke later wrote:

> A stretcher party was passing the trench at the time. They asked if we had a 'passenger' to go back. They took a wounded Officer, but he seemed so badly hit, you would not think he would last out as far as the C.C.S. [Casualty Clearing Station]. This was Major Frank Buckley!

The Major, having received a 'Blighty One' (that is, a wound serious enough for him to be sent back to Britain, or 'dear old Blighty' as home was affectionately called), was transported to a military hospital in Kent. After operating on him, surgeons removed the shrapnel but found that his lungs had been badly punctured. Thanks to his general fitness he eventually made a good recovery but this took a long time and he was in receipt of a war disability pension for some years after the Armistice of November 1918.

After a long spell in hospital and while still recovering, the Major was given a Home Service Commission. His role was now to involve undertaking administrative duties for the Army in the Kent area and he worked very closely with many Canadian troops; he actually fought alongside them at their most famous First World War battle, Vimy Ridge, in 1917. While in Kent with them, Buckley soon became quite a celebrity when it was discovered that he was an England international from the Footballers' Battalion. He wrote with fond recollections of this time, 'They [Canadian soldiers] were very keen on "soccer" and questioned me constantly about the many great players I knew. They greatly appreciated things and could relate to their favourites.'

During his period of convalescence, Franklin Buckley became something of a social celebrity in Kent. His photograph appeared in newspapers and the 'gallant Major' was assigned a Private to act as his chauffeur and batman. He undertook his duties and the social round travelling in a motorcycle sidecar. During this time he became acquainted with such famous people as the writer Thomas Hardy, author of *Tess of the D'Urbervilles* and *Far from the Madding Crowd*, who along with other literary giants of the day, such as J.M. Barrie and Rudyard Kipling, was doing much to raise funds for the Red Cross.

By 17 November 1916 the Battle of the Somme had been officially declared as over. It has been estimated that the six-and-a-half miles the British had advanced in total during the battle had cost a man's life for every yard taken. With such losses the British government had been forced to introduce conscription, as every man was needed at the Front. Even men recovering from wounds were rushed back into service and by the Christmas of 1916 it was felt that Frank Buckley had recovered sufficiently to return to his battalion.

His second stint at the Front started quietly enough when on 3 January 1917 he watched a football match between his fellow officers of the 17th and their opposite numbers in his old regiment (The King's). Not surprisingly, the footballers won 6-1. Sadly this respite was over quickly and the following day the men were back at the Front. They had been practising a new scheme of attack, which was being trialled with a view to it being used in a major spring offensive. The battalion attacked German positions at Argenvillers. In the hand-to-hand fighting that ensued, Buckley distinguished himself so much that his name was specifically recorded for a second time in the report on the fighting later sent to headquarters. To be 'Mentioned in Dispatches' was a great honour, but to have it happen twice is true testament to Frank Buckley's tenacity and bravery.

However, the use of gas and cordite from the shells during the fighting had a greater effect on Frank than on troops in better health, and he was unable to remain at the Front. He was again sent back to England and he spent the remainder of the war working for the Army in Kent.

The fighting of the First World War ended on 11 November 1918 and it left a whole generation changed forever. Frank Buckley later spoke little of the terrible sights he had seen in France but Eddie Holding, who was to played for Buckley at both Wolves and Walsall, recalled the Major describing the carnage he witnessed in a small French village on the battlefront. He also wrote that by the mid-1930s 500 of the battalion's original 600 men were dead, having either been killed in action or dying from wounds suffered during the fighting.

Still suffering from wounds to his lungs, and at over thirty-six years of age, Frank Buckley could no longer make a living playing football. He said the end of the war had left him 'high and dry'. Ever restless, it was time for him to look for new ventures.

FOUR

TANGERINES AND GOLF!

Like so many others, the First World War had left Frank
Buckley a completely changed man. His experiences of
what he termed 'the mud-laden, blood-soaked battle pitches
of France' were to stay in his mind forever, and he genuinely
mourned and always regretted the loss of 'some of the finest
players the game has ever known'. These men had been not
only his comrades but also his friends, and the losses that the
battalion had suffered had indeed been terrible. Over 500 men
of the original 17th Middlesex had been injured or killed.
They were so few in number in the final year of hostilities that
the battalion was disbanded and the remaining men sent to
other units. The decimation of the ranks of footballers generally
is well illustrated when examining the experience of Frank
Buckley's final pre-war club, Bradford City. Of the eleven players in the Bradford team for which he played in 1914, a staggering nine had died in the fighting. These included England
international Jimmy Speirs, who was team captain and a former
FA Cup winner who lost his life at Passchendale in August

1917. Another casualty from that team was the Scottish international Gerald Kirk, who also died fighting for his country.

Surviving former members of the 17th Battalion of the Middlesex Regiment met on occasion and played in charity matches, but Buckley, their second-in-command, never took part in these. His wounds and general poor health restricted him to the sidelines.

Frank had also suffered family bereavement because of the war. His nephew Bernard Buckley, the only surviving son of his eldest brother Benjamin, had died in combat on the Western Front in early June 1917. He lies buried in the British Military Cemetery at Neuvlle-Bournjonval on the Franco-Belgium border. The war had cost both Frank and the nation dear, and distractions were needed to take people's minds off the horrors of the last four years. Sport was to provide such distraction.

The end of the war saw a huge growth of interest in football. The British people, so weary after four years of hardship and fighting, turned to the game for the entertainment and excitement football could always provide. 'Victory Leagues' were formed and professional clubs set about re-establishing themselves. Young players, who had learnt skills and expertise from older players while in the Forces or munitions factories, now came to the fore. They relished the chance to show the people what they could do on a football pitch. But it was not so for Major Buckley.

The end of the war was difficult for the former player. Having turned thirty-six years of age and still suffering badly from the shrapnel wounds to his lungs, a return to a playing career was out of the question. In fact, he was unable to regain anything like full fitness for a number of years, during which he was obliged to attend monthly medical examinations to see if his claim to a small invalidity pension was still justified. This one-time officer was a proud man. He abhorred being reliant on others for his income and he came to detest the humiliation he associated with the monthly 'Board' examination. This was undertaken by an Army-retained doctor called Bradley at his practice above Walton's Store in Corporation Street, Birmingham. To free himself from this detested situation, Major Buckley sought work almost as soon as the war was over and he was free from military responsibilities.

Ideally, Frank Buckley wanted a position with some sort of status and responsibility. Thus the organisational, leadership and management skills he had gleaned from his time in football and the Army could be utilised fully. He could have returned to farming but the condition of his health would have made such physical labour impossible. And even if he had been able, he would no longer have been in partnership with his brother. Christopher Buckley had given up working on the land during the war years. After finishing his playing career with the Villa, Christopher had been employed by Herbert Austin at his Longbridge works. The factory had been adapted for the production of weapons and munitions during hostilities and Christopher's home at Hawksley Farm in south Birmingham had been used to site wooden bungalows imported from Canada to house Longbridge workers. Christopher stayed with the Austin company after the First World War had finished and eventually became the firm's international sales director. His second son Dennis became a racing driver for the Austin company and took part in the Le Mans 24-Hour Endurance Race. He later moved to the United States where he took on an Austin dealership in Los Angeles. He was very successful in this venture and lived on Rodeo Avenue in Hollywood. Dennis Buckley counted many famous film stars of the time as his neighbours.

Because he was in receipt of an Army disability pension, technically Frank Buckley remained on the Army officer reserve list well into the 1920s. However, he must have thought his chance of meaningful employment had come in the spring of 1919. Sir Henry Norris, a director of Arsenal Football Club, approached him with a view to taking over as manager of the Gunners. An interview was arranged between the two men at the Imperial Hotel in Birmingham's city centre to discuss the proposal. Also at the meeting was William Hall, who was a member of the Football League management committee at the time as well as also being an Arsenal director.

Whether or not the post would have been too onerous for Buckley considering his health and the magnitude and importance of the club, he did not take up Norris and Hall's offer of the manager's job. Buckley wrote that he had been unhappy about 'certain issues' that had been discussed at the meeting. He did not elaborate on what these were. His first chance at football management had gone, although his refusal probably led to the eventual appointment of the Arsenal's most famous pre–Second World War manager, Herbert Chapman.

William Hall, Arsenal director.

Buckley became quite despondent, especially as there seemed to be no immediate alternative opportunities of work presenting themselves. To add to his problems, doctors at the medical board insisted that Buckley's health would only improve if he 'settled somewhere near the sea' where the quality of the air would aid his breathing. Without a job, this would have been all but impossible for the Major, but help was at hand.

During the First World War Frank Buckley had developed a close friendship with Frederick Wall, one of the founders of the Footballers' Battalion in 1914. Wall, believed by many to be the inspiration behind Lowe's caricature of English eccentricity, Colonel Blimp, was a member of the Football Association's management committee. He had been active in investigating various bribery scandals that had rocked the sport in the years before football 'shut down' for the duration of the war. He was involved in resolving a particularly notorious affair when, in 1915, Liverpool players had been bribed to 'throw' a cup match against Manchester United. This resulted in several players serving very lengthy bans.

In early March 1919, Wall told Frank Buckley that Norwich City were on the lookout for a manager. The club was attempting to re-establish itself in the Southern League. Football had been kept alive in Norwich during the war by the club playing friendlies. Many of these games were hopelessly one-sided with the Canaries reaching double figures on no fewer than seven occasions. By 1919 they were in dire straits and debt-ridden City were officially wound up at an extraordinary general meeting of the shareholders. However, at a meeting at the Great Eastern Hotel in Norwich on 15 February 1919, a new club was constituted, and a new manager sought. Alerted by Wall, the Major contacted a director of the Norwich City board named John Pyke and offered his services to the club. After a brief interview, Buckley was appointed manager of the Canaries, and was even offered a house on one of Pyke's large estates. This property was close to the famous wetlands, the Norfolk Broads, and in Buckley's own words, 'it provided a climate bracing enough for anyone's requirements'.

Norwich took on Frank Buckley's FA registration from Bradford City, the last club he had turned out for before joining the Middlesex Regiment. Technically he had been on Bradford's books during the period of football close-down during hostilities. By adopting his player registration and becoming his employer, Norwich City were able call on his services as coach and manager. They had no intention of using him as a player. Although far less daunting than taking over at Arsenal, managing Norwich was not without its share of problems, but Frank Buckley set about tackling them with great enthusiasm and energy.

At that time Norwich City played in the most unusual football ground in Britain. Entitled 'The Nest', the Canaries' home ground was situated in a former chalk quarry. A high rock face came within three feet of the pitch. Shots that went wide of the goal rebounded back onto the field of play off the 50ft-high concrete wall that had been built to shore up the chalk face. When Frank Buckley arrived, The Nest was pretty well derelict, having had little maintenance for almost the whole of the war years. More importantly, the new Norwich City Football Club could not field a full team of players when Buckley took over. To add to the difficulties, the Major had to try and build a team under the severest of financial constraints – the team had to be established for 'as little cost as possible'. Thriving under the challenge facing him, Buckley's health started to improve and he went about the task with a will. He scoured the East Midlands area around Nottingham and as far north as Sheffield for promising young players. He was able to sign several for no financial outlay whatsoever. To get information on a player who might benefit the Canaries, Buckley relied on tips and advice from his old Army comrades who lived in various areas around Britain. This country-wide 'scouting' network, which he was to call upon time and again during his long managerial career, was the envy of many, as his scouts were all former players and knew what to look for in a young footballer. It was to become common that if the Major wanted a young player for a position that needed filling, 'all eyes were peeled'. And it paid dividends!

They say 'success breeds success' and that was true of Norwich under Major Buckley. Although beaten 5-0 by Darlington in the cup, the club finished a very commend-able thirteenth in what was to be the final season of the Southern League. Attendances rose and consequently so did gate receipts. Within a year the club were able to spend £4,000 on new changing rooms for the players, whereas Buckley had said that less than twelve months before, 'they would not have been justified in spending as many shillings on such improvements'.

Despite the success he had brought to the Canaries, Frank Buckley only stayed at Carrow Road for one season. In April 1920 an illegal approach was made to tempt one of the Norwich players away. Although he never made public the name of the offending club, he felt the matter was important enough to make a complaint to the game's ruling body, the Football Association. In the controversy that followed, Buckley felt that he was not being fully supported by all the Norwich board of directors. The situation led to a deep split in the Norwich board and team. Major Buckley and a number of players left the club. Five Norwich directors, including the chairman, William Blyth, supported Buckley's stance and also resigned from the club.

Frank Buckley left Norwich 'well on the road to recov-ery'. During his time there he had sold for a large fee a player that he had brought to the club. Samuel Jennings, a former miner from Basford, brought Norwich a very healthy profit.

Buckley appreciated the ball skills this teenager possessed and predicted he would 'become the new Steve Bloomer'. However, although he gained some national fame when playing for Reading and later West Ham, Jennings never reached the same height of fame as Bloomer.

His time at Norwich, although brief, had given the Major a taste of management and indicated an approach to the game that would become his hallmark. He relished the challenge of taking a club that was badly underachieving and setting it on the road to success. Despite being in a better state due to Frank Buckley's efforts, the Canaries did experience some problems after he left. In 1922 the barriers that restrained the crowd on the cliff top at The Nest gave way, but fortunately no one was injured. The club struggled on at this ground for another decade, when subsidence led to a partial pitch collapse and players had to be warned to take particular care when taking corner kicks! Undoubtedly to everyone's relief, the Canaries finally moved to their present home ground at Carrow Road in 1935.

Buckley stated his attitude to management very clearly:

> I visualise that the men who possess the ability to discover, coach and develop young players would eventually have no difficulty whatsoever in disposing of the 'finished product' for lucrative transfer fees.

Buckley clearly understood that post–First World War football would be significantly different from its pre-1914 forerunner. From now on it was purely a business – a business of mass entertainment. It was a business that would thrive, not merely survive by its ability to generate finances. But for Buckley, putting this again into practice was for the future.

Somewhat disillusioned by his experience at Norwich, Buckley now turned his hand to a completely new venture that was to take him out of football for the next three years.

Between 1920 and 1923 the Major worked as a commercial traveller for a confectionary manufacturer based in London. Employed by Maskell's Ltd of Brixton Road to sell sweets to various retailers, Buckley travelled widely in the North of England. He and Madge moved into rented accommodation in the capital, although Frank Buckley was often away from home for days at a time. Frank was initially a great success at his new calling. His personal integrity, dignified appearance and military title impressed his customers and he made good commission earnings. By now he had lost all trace of a Mancunian accent and his officer's bearing presented him as articulate and charming – good qualities for a salesman. However, the good times were not to last!

By early 1923 the economic situation in Britain was starting to decline. The initial boost in production that had followed the cessation of hostilities, when shortfalls from the war years had to be replenished, and the accompanying prosperity for workers was over. Economic recession loomed. With folk having less money to spend on non-essentials and luxuries such as confectionary, Buckley's earnings slumped. Added to this, his health was again deteriorating from the hectic pace of life he was experiencing and from living in the polluted atmosphere of London. He needed a change and, as luck would have it, he was drawn back into football by a chance meeting he had on a northbound train in early 1923.

It was while travelling to Blackpool to sell his wares that Major Frank Buckley bumped into Albert Hargreaves. The Major knew Hargreaves well. Hargreaves had been a football referee before the First World War. As they reminisced about football and characters from the old days, Hargreaves revealed that he was a director of Blackpool Football Club, and that the Seasiders were looking for a manager. Showing great interest, Hargreaves invited Buckley to meet Blackpool's president, Sir Lansay Parkinson, 'over a cup of tea'. After what he described as a 'momentous meeting' Buckley was appointed Blackpool's manager for the start of the 1923/24 season. The Buckleys already had family connections in the Blackpool area: the Major's older brother Edward Alfred Buckley lived in the town and made a living selling mortgages for the Halifax Building Society. Blackpool had also been the location for the family floor-laying firm.

Blackpool FC was a solid club that had been around since well before the war. It had developed a reputation for playing football that was considered adequate but rather 'plodding' and uninspiring. In fact, their usual fare at the time the Major took the reins has been described as 'anonymous and fuss free'. This is not to say the club had not had players of note, who had gained fame for their artistry and individualism. One such was George Mee, an inside forward, who had turned out for a record 195 consecutive games. Tragically, a fellow player of Mee's, a gifted full-back named Peter Fairhurst, had collapsed in a coma after heading a rain-soaked football in a League match. Sadly he did not regain consciousness and died of brain damage.

Upon taking control of the club, Buckley realised the magnitude of the problems he was faced with. Having being formed in 1877 as a church-based football outfit called the Victoria Club, Blackpool had had little success over the years. In truth, its image was boring and expectations of future success were almost non-existent. Frank Buckley set about changing this.

His first action was to introduce some panache into the side. He abandoned Blackpool's traditional strip and brought in players' shirts of a bright orange, or 'tangerine' as it became known. The psychological effect of this simple act on the grey football world of the 1920s was dramatic and caused many eyebrows to be raised. In the true spirit of the 'roaring twenties', Buckley was challenging people to perceive Blackpool Football Club as bright and vibrant, a football club for the 'new age' – the 'Motor age' – the age where 'anything goes'! Not that the changes he wrought stopped with what some might say were superficial alterations in kit. Buckley reactivated the network of scouting contacts he had used while at Norwich. He set in place a system that would serve Blackpool well after the Major had moved on to fresh pastures. Perhaps the most important acquisition made by Buckley in his first season with the 'Seasiders' was the signing of Jimmy Hampson from non-League Nelson FC for a fee of £2,000. In his first season with Blackpool, Hampson scored 31 goals and within three years he had amassed a staggering 116 goals for the club. By 1931 Hampson was a full England international, and he remained Blackpool's greatest asset throughout the 1930s. Undoubtedly Hampson would have had a career in football management after the Second World War had he not been tragically drowned in a fishing accident off the Fleetwood coast in 1938.

A strange event took place while Buckley was in charge at Blackpool. He had heard good reports from Rotherham concerning two young full-backs that were playing for Treeton Miners Welfare Club. Ever ready to seize the opportunity to sign good quality players, Buckley offered both players full-time contracts after he had watched them play. One of the lads accepted the offer, but the other refused, fearing the loss of seemingly secure but low-paid work in the pits. Over twenty years later the Major met this man again while he was attempting to sign a young soldier named Jesse Pye for Notts County. The Treeton miner who had refused Buckley's offer turned out to be Jesse Pye's father! Pye junior (who was later to score for Wolves in the 1949 FA Cup final) was reluctant to sign for County at the time, but was persuaded when his father said, 'Mr Buckley, I think I made a mistake all those years ago. I should have joined you. Jesse lad – don't make the same mistake!' Jesse duly signed for the Major, who later joked, 'I missed the father, but I got the son!'

With a strong belief in maintaining high levels of physical fitness, Buckley put his players on strict orders as to what they could eat and drink. They were under instruction to have early nights two days prior to a fixture and not to socialise during this time. He changed training practices and would personally referee practice games where he could simultaneously coach his young charges. He conducted research into the comparatively new area of physiotherapy and, applying such measures, Buckley soon gained a reputation for getting injured players back to fitness in relatively short time.

Important events happened on the domestic front while Major Buckley was at Blackpool. In May 1924 his son Jack married Edith Newall. Jack Buckley had not followed his father into either football or farming. Instead he had become quite a sought-after motorcycle mechanic. He attended a number of Isle of Man TT races during the 1920s where he serviced and repaired motorcycles. The growth in this form of motor sport after the First World War was swift and dramatic as motorcycling became immensely popular. It seems Jack Buckley was more gifted in practical matters than financial ones and he allowed many riders to run up large bills for jobs he had done for them. Not all his debtors paid up and eventually Jack got into financial difficulties. A family story has it that he turned to his father for help. Asking for ten or twenty pounds to tide him over, Jack was hurt and disappointed when the Major refused. Buckley senior believed in the value of 'self help' and reasoned that if Jack had got himself into a financial mess, he could get himself out. This led to a schism between father and son and there was little contact between them until Frank Buckley's later years. Like others in his extended family, Jack Buckley eventually became a motor car salesman, and for many years ran a successful business in Herefordshire. However, despite the difficulties he had with the Major, Jack christened his eldest son Franklin after his father. This grandson of the Major eventually became a doctor in London.

Jack Buckley and wife Edith in 1924. (Mrs M. Powell and family collection)

The success Blackpool enjoyed in the years after Buckley left was due in large measure to the practices he established. By the mid-1930s the Seasiders had lost their 'average' and 'uninspiring' tag, and had gained promotion to the First Division. It has even been said that the achievements of the 1950s, when they won the cup, were due in no small part to the work Major Buckley had put in establishing the image and self-esteem of Blackpool Football Club.

Among the other influential players the Major brought on for the Seasiders included a winger called Davies who was not to miss a game for the club in over five years. A forward called Tremelling, whose brother was a goalkeeper for Birmingham, was also a fine Buckley discovery. Tremelling scored 74 goals for Blackpool at both first and reserve team level in a single season, despite suffering a broken leg halfway through!

Although Blackpool gained a great deal from Buckley's time with them, it was not all one-way traffic. He benefited too. The reversion to living in a coastal area with good clear air had a remarkable effect on the Major. His health improved no end and he even took up a new sport; on the advice of his younger brother Chris, the Major started playing golf. He soon developed great skill at this game that gave him a good excuse to enjoy the 'great outdoors' at Lytham St. Annes. Throughout his life, Frank always had a very close relationship with his brother Christopher. It says something of the strength of their family bonds that when Chris's wife (and Frank's stepdaughter) Mignon gave birth to a son in January 1911, the couple named him Franklyn Charles Buckley in honour of the Major. Unlike the Major's own son, who had been born some six years earlier, this Frank Buckley junior followed in the family's military tradition by becoming Company Quarter Sergeant Major while in the Officer Training Corps at King Edward's School, Birmingham, in the 1920s. He was

Frank and Madge Buckley (left), 1924. (Mrs M. Powell and family collection)

commissioned as an officer in the regular Army in July 1939. He served in various theatres of war and eventually reached the exalted rank of Lieutenant Colonel in the Royal Army Ordinance Corps. Christopher became a senior car sales executive with Austin when he retired from football and eventually became a member of the board of directors of the motor company. He kept an interest in football by becoming chairman of Aston Villa in the 1960s but sadly lost one of his daughters in a car accident while she was driving him home after a match at Villa Park. Although he had lived at Hawkesley Farm in Northfield in Birmingham during the First World War he moved when Herbert Austin developed the site into a village to house workers making munitions at his Longbridge Factory. The Austin company purchased St Leonard's Grange at Beoley, north of Redditch, for Christopher Buckley and his family. He lived there until his death in 1973.

Within a year of taking up golf, Major Buckley had become the Lytham club champion and by 1927 he was a regular entrant in the annual Lancashire Full Amateur Championship. It became a great joke with him to invite guests to join him on the tees at 6 a.m. with the intention of completing a full eighteen-hole round before breakfast. He said generally two invitations 'finished guests off'.

With his health fully restored, Frank Buckley turned his thoughts to moving on again and he sought a bigger challenge. In 1927 he became aware of a troubled sleeping giant in the world of football; a club that was desperate for a Moses figure, a man of vision, inspiration and ideas to lead them back to the heights of the English game.

The giant was Wolverhampton Wanderers. The man was Franklin Buckley.

FIVE

WAKING THE WOLF

In April 1927, in what was a rare act of unity, the board of directors at Wolverhampton Wanderers decided that new blood was desperately needed to drive the club forward.

Unlike other places such as Bristol or Sheffield, Wolverhampton, a prosperous Black Country manufacturing town for over a century, boasted only one football team – the Wolves! Formed in 1877 at St Luke's School in the Blakenhall area of the town, Wolves had been one of the founder members of the Football League at its inception in 1888. Prior to 1927, the club had had a chequered history, having been FA Cup finalists on five occasions and winners twice. On the downside it had spent well over half its life in the lower divisions. There is no doubt that the people of the town were as passionate about their football then as they are now and not slow in demonstrating it. An example of this was when Wolves were banned from playing at Molineux for two months in the autumn of 1919 because of crowd trouble. They were forced to play their matches at The Hawthorns of all places – the home of their fierce local rivals West Bromwich Albion! By 1927, the year of its

Golden Jubilee, Wolves had had only four managers, and three of those had served in the last five years. These men, who all combined the role of club secretary with that of team manager, had shaped the club up until then, and they were a pretty mixed bunch.

The longest serving by far was John Addenbroke, who had been with the club for thirty-seven years. Known as Jack, Addenbroke could trace his association back to being a twenty-year-old teacher at the home of Wolves' predecessor club, St Luke's School. He oversaw Wolves' entry into the League in 1888 and their first Molineux game against Villa a year later. Under Addenbroke, Wolves had had their FA Cup successes and enjoyed stability, but sadly he fell ill and died in the summer of 1922 at the comparatively young age of fifty-seven. His passing marked the end of an era.

Addenbroke's death forced Wolves to look elsewhere for a manager. An ex-professional player from the North-East named George Jobey was appointed to run the team. Jobey, who had played for Arsenal and had the distinction of scoring the first ever goal at Highbury in 1913, had very mixed fortunes in the two years he was to be at Wolves. During his first season in charge they were relegated to the Third Division (North) for the first time in the club's history, having won only 9 games out of 42 played.

This relegation was to be a watershed in Wolves' history. Finishing seventeenth in the Second Division and with local support draining away, the famous old-gold-and-black club was all but bankrupt. At the club's AGM of that year, debts totalling £3,885 were declared and the existing management company was immediately wound up. However, a new company, Wolverhampton Wanderers (1923), was floated straight away, with shares initially totalling a value of £5,000, although it had a declared nominal capital of £30,000. The new company was fronted by a retired Army major called Holloway and the reconstituted

board was headed by Ernest Barker, who earned his living
as a local corn merchant. The initial share issue was well
over-subscribed by wealthy supporters and a fresh issue was
ordered. Eventually, £8,402 was invested in the club. The
first act of the new company was to buy the freehold of the
Molineux ground from Northampton Brewery Company
for £5,607. This brewery had owned the former pleasure
gardens since the late 1880s and had converted Molineux
House into a hotel. The company had helped Wolves a lot
when the club moved there in 1889.

With a new start for the club, Wolves gained promotion back to the Second Division at their first attempt. The
club celebrated this by the issue of new shirts to the players, which incorporated a large black 'V' (for Victory) set
on the traditional old-gold background. It is interesting to
speculate if Prime Minister Winston Churchill 'pinched'
this idea for his iconic 'V for Victory' slogan and symbol of
the Second World War.

Despite this renewed enthusiasm that had brought success
on the field, the board of directors suffered great upheaval
that season because of three deaths from among its members. At the end of the season a strong pressure group called
'the Shareholders Club', which had been formed as far back
as 1911 to raise funds but also to monitor the football club's
management, began to question things. This group had tra-
ditionally been made up of supporters who were not part
of the Wolves' directorship. So great was their disquiet they
even managed to have two of their members (men called
Walsh and Poulton) elected onto the board. Major Buckley
believed the existence of the Shareholders Club was a factor
in ensuring continuing disunity among those charged with
ensuring Wolves' progress. Drawn by the offer of a better
deal, Jobey left Wolves to manage Derby County. Apart from
the promotion, his greatest legacy to the Wolves was the
acquisition of Tom Phillipson from Swindon. Phillipson was

to score over 100 goals for the club. Jobey did well for Derby between 1924 and 1941, and attracted some fine players to the Rams. However, in 1941 an FA Committee sitting in the town found that he had made illegal payments to players and fraudulently disguised the fact in the club's accounts. Derby County were fined £500 and Jobey was banned from football for life. Although the ban was rescinded in 1945, he was never again a significant figure in football management.

After Jobey's departure in 1924, the club turned 'in-house' to seek a replacement. The directors appointed a local man from Tettenhall named Albert Hoskins. This was an uncontroversial and 'safe' appointment that did not antagonise the warring factions on the board of directors. Hoskins, a very popular figure around Molineux, had been associated with Wolves for almost a quarter of a century since having player trials in 1900. Four years later he had been taken on as a clerk at the club and had served in most administrative capacities at Molineux – including receptionist and ticketseller – up until his appointment as secretary/manager in May 1924. Despite being considered by many to lack the experience necessary to bring success to the club, Hoskins' control of the reins was steady and Wolves finished as high as fourth in the Second Division. However, a stronger character was sought to bring First Division football to Wolverhampton in the 1926/27 season and the directors looked for an experienced man. The Stockport County manager, a tough Lancastrian called Fred Scotchbrook, was given the keys to the manager's office at Molineux.

Briefly a professional player with Bolton Wanderers in 1914, Fred Scotchbrook had had his career curtailed by the First World War. The fifteen months he was at the helm in Wolverhampton can only be described as acrimonious. The start of his period in charge had promised much. The club had opened a state-of-the-art new stand on the Waterloo Road side of the ground and had covered the 'cowshed', or North Bank as it was properly known. Expectations for the forthcoming season were high. However, things went wrong very quickly and Scotchbrook complained bitterly of the directors' lack of financial support for his dealings on the transfer market and their general interference in team affairs. Matters came to a head at the club's AGM in 1927 when he stated that Wolves would have won the cup had he been allowed to purchase a quality centre half to shore up their leaky defence. Scotchbrook did as well as he could considering the divisions in the boardroom that he had to deal with. He had managed to get the club up to fourth place in the Second Division, having amassed 49 points. However, Wolves' finances were again in a mess, having a bank overdraft of nearly £14,800 and mounting yearly losses. Annual gate receipts of £15,000 could barely meet the club's wage bill and running costs. Although the club had made modest profits at the end of the 1923 and 1924 seasons, by 1927 Wolves had lost over £1,500 in a single year. Much of this can be accounted for in a deficit in the transfer market of some £2,625. Wolves simply could not finance the purchase of the new players that Scotchbrook wanted, and after further heated exchanges between himself and two directors, he walked out of the club.

So it was that Ernest Barker, on behalf of the whole board, advertised for a replacement for Scotchbrook at the end of the 1926/27 season. Over sixty men of varying experience and ability wrote to Barker about the vacancy, but after the applications had been sifted through, only one man was invited for interview – Major Frank Buckley.

Frank Buckley arrived at Wolverhampton High Level Station on the train from Blackpool late in the afternoon of Monday 23 May 1927. He was met by Ernest Barker and a couple of the other Wolves directors. Over a pot of tea and several rounds of toast in the restaurant of the Victoria Hotel, Buckley's proposed appointment was discussed.

It is not hard to see why Frank Buckley made an ideal candidate for the Wolves managerial position. His experience at both Blackpool and Norwich of acquiring skilled and talented players at little or no cost and then selling them on at a healthy profit was extremely appealing to those concerned with club finances. Considering Wolves' plight, this message was not lost on Barker and his colleagues. But there were other reasons why Buckley would be a good appointment at Wolves. From his military experience in leading men, Frank Buckley had the knowledge and strength of character to tackle the factionalism and polarity that was so bedevilling the running of Wolves. The local newspaper referred to the Major as 'on all counts a personality' and his bearing and steely eyed stare made anyone who stood against his resolve either very brave or very foolish! He also offered Wolves a planned approach to getting them a place of prominence in the world of football. In almost military terms, he described to the board a five-year plan – five years in which a whole new team and its support network could be established and a culture of success be embedded at Molineux. However, not least of all, he offered the Wolves directors a 'no-lose' guarantee. Upon being appointed, he said that if they were not happy with his efforts after a year 'they were to kick me out'.

Buckley later recalled the interview. Ernest Barker had been very honest in describing the situation at the club and Buckley wrote of his impressions of the meeting: 'Wolverhampton Wanderers were in a poor state both financially and from a playing point of view. I listened carefully and felt "here is a man's job indeed!" but I also felt it was worthwhile.' At the end of the meeting his initial appointment on a three-year contract was unanimously approved at an annual salary of £650 per year commencing on 1 June 1927.

Frank Buckley was genuinely pleased to be at Wolves. He was interviewed by the local paper the *Express and Star* a week after his appointment and he stated that he 'had many happy recollections of hard struggles at Molineux Grounds' as a player and as manager of Blackpool. He also said proudly that he 'considered it a great honour to go to a club [Wolves] with such a record'. However, he was well aware of the situation he was faced with. He later wrote, 'that famous old club Wolverhampton Wanderers was in dire trouble and nothing would go right for them. I felt it was my chance!'

Buckley made a quiet start to his regime at Molineux. He introduced himself to the players and staff on 27 July and decided not to make sweeping staff changes right away. Buckley inherited a squad of thirty first-team players, only one of whom had come from the club's junior team. Over half the rest had been signed from non-League clubs. He was well aware that, despite his appointment, the board of directors was still a very volatile group. He had witnessed one of their meetings where 'recriminations were freely flung about and threats made'. The Major distanced himself from this and concentrated on team matters. He had been given the full support of the directors of two of the town's largest commercial concerns – the *Express and Star* and Butler's, the local brewery.

As at Blackpool he introduced a new strip, by way of demarcating the change from the previous management set-up. He designed the shirts himself. The players now would now wear shirts of black and gold stripes, reminiscent of the kit worn by their predecessors in 1908 when Wolves won the FA Cup. A strong advocate of players having maximum physical fitness, he introduced the training methods he had used at Blackpool. Based on British Army physical instruction, Wolves' players now did exercises with Indian clubs and far more weight training than they had been used to. Regular practice matches were organised in which players would be tried in positions other than their usual roles. These took place with the Major refereeing. This gave him the opportunity to coach players while monitoring their performance. Buckley believed his players should be flexible and versatile. It was not unusual for him to redesignate players to new positions as they were actually going onto the Molineux pitch to play a game!

The Major gave each of his players a small pocket book in which was printed details of the conduct he expected from them. As well as advice on not smoking, he insisted that they did not go out socialising for at least two days prior to a match. This rule was eventually brought to the attention of the Wolverhampton public, and it was not unknown for people to telephone the Major if they saw a player in town on a Thursday or Friday night. It was also said that Buckley scoured the picture houses of the town on occasion looking for errant players. The one or two who had taken the risk had to hide under the cinema seats until he had gone.

In order to keep some continuity the Major wisely kept the same team captain, Phillipson, and also retained as vice-captain Harold Shaw, who had been signed from Swindon by Jobey in 1923. They had both served the club under Hoskins and Scotchbrook. Shaw, a talented full-back who was seriously considered for an England cap, became a great friend of the Major and was taught to play golf by him. Buckley initially stayed in 'digs' in Dunkley Street in the Whitmore Reans area of Wolverhampton, where he was looked after by two elderly sisters, while Madge continued to live in the family home in Blackpool. The Major did not have a car of his own and it became a regular practice for Harold Shaw to drive him back up to Blackpool late on a Saturday afternoon when a game had finished.

Despite this friendship, Shaw wanted First Division football and Buckley had no qualms in selling him to Sunderland two years later for the handsome fee of £7,000. Strangely, the deal was hurried through on a train while Wolves were returning from playing Nottingham Forest. Although Wolves' directors were very pleased with this income, two of them – men called Oakley and Matthews – complained to the Major later that week that he hadn't signed a replacement. Dramatically, Buckley told them, 'If you drive your car as I direct, I will produce a full-back as good as Shaw.' He added quietly, 'and his name also will be Shaw'. The three drove to Mansfield where a seventeen-year-old miner lived who had been recommended to the Major by one of his old Army pals. This player, Cecil Shaw, was not at home and the Major and his companions found the young man leaving a local cinema. After a brief conversation he duly signed papers for Wolves on the bonnet of Mr Oakley's car in the cinema car park. Cecil Shaw was to play a record 114 consecutive matches for Wolves in the seven years he was at the club and was eventually the team captain.

If anyone expected miracles from Buckley's first season in charge they would have been disappointed. They finished in sixteenth place in the Second Division, one place lower than the previous season, although they had gained one more point. The season is best remembered for the club buying a young Wolverhampton soldier out of the Royal Horse Artillery to play for Wolves. This was the famous Billy Hartill, who had been a prolific scorer for the RHA's football team, hitting the net over 70 times in two seasons. In forthcoming seasons, Hartill (nicknamed 'Hartillery Billy' by the fans because of his military connections) was to score 170 goals in 234 appearances for Wolves and was instrumental in helping them finally achieve promotion in 1932.

The season also marked the final appearance of a very popular Wolves goalkeeper. Noel George, who had been the first-choice 'keeper since 1919, appeared in the old-gold and black over 240 times in the 1920s. Famous for being able to clasp a football in either hand he had been a good servant to the Wolves. Sadly, at the end of the Major's first season in charge, Noel George was diagnosed as being terminally ill with a disease of the gums. Despite money being tight, the board supported George financially after he became too ill to play. He died in 1929 from his illness, which the Major believed was due to ill-fitting dentures. From that time on he made sure that all his players who wore dentures were examined by a dentist every six months!

The 1928/29 season was an even bigger disappointment than Buckley's first year at Wolves. Although the team gained a few more points, they actually finished seventeenth in the Second Division. The lowest point of a very disappointing season was the 1-0 cup defeat at home by lowly non-League Mansfield. Rumour has it that the Major organised a training run through Wolverhampton town centre for the first-team players on a market day during the following week. There is little doubt that the people of Wolverhampton made sure the players knew their opinion of the recent performance!

This season saw the very unpopular sale of the talented Reg Weaver to Chelsea. Weaver, signed by Fred Scotchbrook from Newport in 1927, was a prolific goalscorer (29 goals in 57 games) and a favourite among the fans. However, the Major was objective enough to know that the £5,000 the sale put into the Wanderers' coffers to help keep the club afloat was more important than the sensitivity of popular feeling.

The sale of Weaver and Harold Shaw, both talented players and popular heroes to the Wolves' faithful, was the start of a practice Frank Buckley was to continue throughout his years at Molineux. Preferring to gain publicity rather than popularity, the Major was always pragmatic in his approach to raising finances for the club. Buckley was never afraid to court popular ill-feeling from the supporters if he believed his actions were in Wolves' best interests. The greatest example of this was to come in 1938 with the infamous sale of Bryn Jones to Arsenal for a then-record fee of £14,000. However, the Major always had a more than capable replacement waiting in the wings.

The following season saw the start of a gradual improvement as the team finished in ninth place, although they were knocked out of the FA Cup in the third round by Oldham Athletic, losing 1-0. Even so, the Major declared that 'the sun was starting to shine'. By now, Frank Buckley had transformed the team. Since his arrival at Wolves, seventeen players had retired or moved on to other clubs, while thirteen had been signed, mainly from lower league or amateur sides. Among these early signings was Dai Richards, a defender from Merthyr Town who eventually played 229 times for Wolves and became a Welsh international.

The 1930/31 season saw a dramatic improvement in Wolves' performances. They finished fourth and signed an excellent player in Tom Smalley. Smalley, like Cecil Shaw, was a miner and came from South Kirby Colliery in Yorkshire. Smalley stayed with Wolves for seven years and, in 1936, was the first Molineux man to be capped for England for sixteen years. The 1930/31 season also saw Buckley appoint a former Wolves player, Dick Bradford, to the Wolves' backroom staff. Bradford introduced the new practices of massage, physiotherapy and electric stimulation to the treatment room, ensuring players recovered from injuries and knocks quicker.

Bradford's appointment shows that Buckley took an innovative and scientific approach to looking after his players. He saw them as a considerable financial asset to the club as well as individuals, and Bradford's work was one way of protecting the club's investments.

The 1931/32 season was one of the finest in the club's history. When Billy Hartill put two goals past the Port Vale 'keeper on 23 April the crowd at Molineux went wild and invaded the pitch. Having amassed a staggering 56 points for the season, Wolves were finally promoted to the First Division. It had been a truly great season. The team had scored 115 goals and conceded well less than half that number. In six of their matches they had beaten the opposition by at least five goals and the team boasted several more fine players, including Dickie Rhodes, Deacon, Hollingworth, Kay and another Welsh international, Lumberg. Albert Kay was the only player still in the first team that the Major had inherited from his predecessor, Fred Scotchbrook. Having appeared for Wolves nearly 300 times between 1927 and 1932, Kay never played in the First Division as he retired at the end of the promotion season.

Buckley had given the directors a five-year plan and it had taken the full five years to achieve First Division status. By now the club's finances were strong and the Shareholders Club had fallen by the wayside, making a final donation to the club of £400. Indeed, according to Buckley investors had done well under his stewardship, having received on average seven-and-a-half per cent interest for each year that he had been in charge.

The future in the First Division held many new challenges for Major Buckley. For the first time in his managerial career he was in charge of a team in the top flight. His first task was to keep Wolves there; subsequently he hoped to build the club into one of the strongest in the land. It was a daunting prospect, one which Buckley was to face without his friend Ernest Barker, who died shortly after the sounds of the promotion celebrations faded away.

SIX

DANCES AT WOLVES

On Monday 10 April 1932, the *Express and Star* published a supplement to its usual evening edition. This was a written dedication to the Wolves securing promotion to the First Division by beating Port Vale 2-0 the previous Saturday and contained this tribute to Franklin Buckley:

Major Buckley
The Man at the Wheel
Major Buckley will remember Saturday as one of the Red-Letter days of his life. By his splendid work with the Wolves he has built up a reputation as a football manager second to none in the country.

The Major created a big impression as the Manager of Blackpool when he came to the Wolves. At the Molineux Ground he has proved himself a splendid judge of a player. His ability to find a young talent is unequalled and despite the handicaps with which he is faced when joining the Club he has discovered a whole team, which has taken Wolves into the highest flight.
A great achievement Major Buckley!

The supplement also contained congratulations and tributes from other First Division managers and secretaries. They welcomed Wolves back to the First Division after a twenty-six-year absence, and relished the prospect of their teams playing the men in old-gold and black. Not only had the first team won promotion to the First Division, but the reserves had been crowned champions of the Central League. Among those who sent congratulatory telegrams was the Major's predecessor at Wolves, George Jobey, who was then managing Derby County. Jack Pedley, who had been the Wanderers' left-back at the time they were demoted back in 1906 also sent his good wishes and congratulated the team. The Major organised a presentation fund and with season's profits of £4,123 17s 3d, the overdraft at the bank was finally paid off. On 2 June that year a complimentary dinner was laid on by the town council at the Victoria Hotel. There were speeches praising Wolves given by the mayor, Alderman Levi Johnson, and leading Wolverhampton entrepreneur James Beattie. Among the invited guests was the Reverend Kenneth Hunt, Olympic gold medallist and hero of Wolves' famous cup final victory over Newcastle in 1908.

There was little doubt that Buckley's popularity was at an all-time high and with the opening of the Molineux Street Stand, costing £20,500 and holding 8,000 spectators under cover, the future looked bright for the Wanderers.

Frank Buckley was a realist and knew the team that had won him promotion was not good enough to keep Wolves in the top flight. He wanted more than he had achieved at Norwich and Blackpool, where he had turned around the fortunes of these clubs and then left to go on to fresh challenges. In gaining promotion at Wolves, he had taken a stagnating club and brought stability, success and financial security, but now he wanted more. Buckley was not content with mere survival in the First Division. He dreamed of making his Wolves a power in the land! On the day Wolves had gained promotion, Major Buckley had commented, 'Now they are back in Division one, they are going to stop there!' This intention was going to take more than mere rhetoric. It would require long-term planning, but his immediate priority was to ensure the club survived the first season, when inexperience in the top flight would make Wolves vulnerable to relegation. What a nail-biting season it was!

The Major had not strengthened his team with a great deal of transfer activity during the close season of 1932. He had bought Tom Smalley and goalkeeper Frank Wildman from South Kirby Colliery the year before, but neither had played a great deal during the promotion season. In their first year in the top division, the Major continued to rely on utilising players he had found in non-League football. Nine new men appeared in Wolves' colours during the 1932/33 season, but several of these were to play only a handful of games for the club – Ted Ivil from Little Hutton played 4 times and Tom Wildsmith, signed from Hadfield Sports, turned out for Wolves only once. Wolves failed to get beyond their first game in the FA Cup, losing to Derby County at home 6-3 in January 1934, and Arsenal had put seven past them at home the previous November. After that performance, Buckley sold the first-team goalkeeper, Alf Toothill, to Fulham for £1,000!

As the end of the season approached, Wolves looked odds-on favourites to go straight back down to the Second Division. They had spent most of the season at the bottom of the table but an unexpected 4-2 win over Everton in the final game put them two points above Bolton Wanderers, who joined Blackpool in taking 'the drop'. Wolves had survived but only by the skin of their teeth! However, it had been a very successful season financially. The board declared profits of £7,610, and average gates had almost doubled compared with Buckley's first season at Molineux. In fact, for the remainder of the 1930s while Buckley was in charge, average gates never dipped below 24,000. The growth in support and financial stability gave the club a sound footing for forthcoming campaigns.

Wolves celebrated their survival in the First Division by a pre-season tour overseas. Buckley organised a four-game tournament in France with matches in Paris, Marseilles, Nice and Nimes. The trip was marred by a crowd riot at Nice, and Buckley had no hesitation in taking his team off the field. The team only returned to finish the match when extra French police had been drafted in. Buckley told the *Express and Star*, 'I have brought my team here to play football, not to be slaughtered!' Later, his actions were supported by Fred Wall (who by this time had been knighted), who after reading about the incident contacted the Major and told him, 'You did right, my son.' Surprisingly the incident did not leave bad blood between the clubs; Nice FC visited Molineux the following close season and links continued up until the outbreak of the Second World War.

Their second season in the First Division saw an improvement in Wolves' fortunes. They finished fifteenth in the League and got to the fourth round of the FA Cup, but again were beaten by Derby County. Sir Charles Mander (of the famous local paint-making family) had become club president in 1932, and he awarded six players 'benefits' of £400 each for their loyal service to Wolves. This was a lot of money at the time and would easily buy a brand new detached property with about a quarter of an acre of land locally. It is an indication of how healthy Wolves' finances had become under Major Buckley's regime. In his address, Mander emphasised that no other club had given benefits to so many players at once. Nearly all the men were products of Wolves' own training scheme and not 'imported' from other clubs. These men – Lowton, Hartill, Barraclough, Rhodes, Deacon and

Hollingworth – were said by the Major to be an example to others for 'their application, concentration and self-denial'. The 1933/34 season is perhaps also best remembered for the acquisition of the talented Welsh forward Brynmor Jones from Aberaman for £1,500. Bryn Jones had had an unsuccessful trial with Southend, where his brother Emlyn was a professional. He had a second brother, Ivor, who was on the books of local rivals West Bromwich Albion. Bryn was small in stature, measuring 5ft 6ins and weighing only 11st. He scored on average a goal every three games during his five years at Wolves and initially stood in for Hartill. It was to be Jones' transfer to Arsenal in 1938 that would see Buckley at his most unpopular among the Wolves' faithful.

It was also in 1933 that, for the first time in his career as manager of Wolves, Armistice Day, 11 November, fell on a Saturday with Wolves playing Arsenal at home. Major Buckley not only insisted on wearing his own military decorations from the First World War during the match as an act of remembrance and respect to his fallen comrades; he also encouraged supporters who had seen active service to do likewise. Proudly bearing the 1914/15 star, the 'War' medal (with two oak leaves on the ribbon representing the times he had been Mentioned in Dispatches) and the golden 'Victory' medal, Buckley was warmly applauded as he made his way to the home dugout at the start of the game. Many men in the crowd also wore these three decorations, which were popularly called 'Pip, Squeak and Wilfred' after cartoon characters. Although Wolves lost the match 1-0, there was a lot of pride at Molineux that day.

It was in 1934 that Frank Buckley actually acquired a car of his own. He was now living at a house on the edge of Wolverhampton called 'The Haven' during the week and he bought an Austin 16 York Saloon from Don Everall's garage near the Gaumont cinema on Snow Hill. His brother Christopher actually worked for Austin and eventually became their managing director. Major Buckley would have used this stylish little car to travel to his weekend abode at Island Pool.

In the 1930s a fortnightly visit to Molineux became a 'must' for many Wulfrunians. It became commonplace for whole families to attend matches, as soccer was changing from being a totally male preserve. A locally born lifelong supporter, Alan Meddings, recalled those long-ago days. He said that on home match days he and his parents would meet family friends at Molineux and take their regular places at the old 'cowshed' (North Bank) end of the ground. The men would stand at the edge of the group so as to form a barrier around the women in the party. This protected them a little from being pushed and shoved about by the crowd. Mr Meddings added that even when the crowd were in a frenzy of excitement, bad language would not be tolerated, and anyone heard swearing would be 'turned on' by the crowd. There was an element of gentility about match days. Tea, and later coffee, was served in china cups and saucers, and many people would dress smartly for matches. A lasting impression of Mr Meddings was of the sweet sellers (ground staff known as 'chocolate boys'), who ambled around the pitch selling their wares before the start of a game and at half-time. He recalled that children (who could not easily move because of the crowd) would shout their order to a 'chocolate boy' and throw their two pennies for him to collect. 'With mind-blowing accuracy' the sweets would be thrown back to the children. Mr Meddings said he was always amazed that the sweets always arrived straight back to the right person, despite the big crowd surrounding them. (If only all footballers could aim as straight!)

Alan Meddings remembers looking forward to home matches and seeing the 'stars' from each visiting team. He looks back very fondly on the days at Wolves when Major Buckley was in charge.

Many fans of the time, like Mr Meddings, will recall the unofficial half-time 'entertainment' of the time, provided by a local man called Dickie Westwood. Mr Westwood, who earned his living as a coalman, would climb onto the pitch at half-time, often apparently inebriated. Wearing two small oranges and a piece of black pudding pinned to the lapel of his jacket (showing his support for the old-gold and black of the Wolves), Dickie would remove his flat cap and kick it around one of the goalmouths, demonstrating to the crowd how the Wolves forwards should be playing. To a tremendous roar, he would complete his demonstration by kicking his hat into the back of the net! He would then put his hat back on and quietly go back to his place on the terraces without any bother. It seems that Mr Westwood was a well-known figure 'down the Wolves' before and after the Second World War.

So it can be seen that gradually the culture of football support in Wolverhampton grew strong in the 1930s as Major Buckley bought success to the club.

Some supporters would cycle to Molineux on the 'sit-up-and-beg' bikes of the time, often with an excited young son perched precariously on the crossbar as they flew down Wadham's Hill. For a penny ('payable on arrival'), their bike would be left for the duration of the game in the backyard of someone living in the warren of little backstreets that surrounded the ground. Another local man, Bob Sadler, also remembers those times:

> My father was a fanatical supporter, and I remember the crowds hurrying to get to the Molineux. They went in their droves, trotting at times to overtake each other, like rats following the Pied Piper! At home, after the match, the family and two Wolves reserve players (both Scots called Rennie and McLaine) who were in digs close by, would sit around the kitchen table and go through a minute-by-minute inquest into the game.

By the mid-1930s Wolves boasted several full international players and Buckley's policy of 'find 'em young and sell 'em on' was at its height. A whole stream of recruits came through the Molineux doors to be assessed, trained and coached if good enough. Wolves' fans never always fully understood why young players who had potential were sold to other clubs and it was even said that some local wag wrote in the dust on the back of the youth team bus 'Stop me and buy one'! Buckley knew what he was doing. As in the case of the two Shaws, Harold and Cecil, the previous decade, he always had a more-than-adequate replacement waiting in the wings when a player was sold. The frenetic pace of player acquisition and disposal was evident by the fact that in 1936 only seven of the season's thirty-five professionals had been with the club more than three years. In finding his new players, the Major would use his network of scouts to search high and low. In December 1934, he went across to Ireland with the express blessing of the directors to 'specifically purchase a right-back, irrespective of the cost'. He returned with a centre forward, an inside forward and a goalkeeper! The centre forward was Dave Martin. Nicknamed 'Boy', Martin was a player of international quality who scored a very impressive 18 goals in 27 appearances in old-gold and black before transferring to Nottingham Forest in 1937.

The 1933/34 season saw Wolves slip to seventeenth place in the First Division but at least the team's status as a top-flight outfit was secure. The campaign saw the start of Buckley's building of a team capable of attaining titles and silverware. Old regulars such as Barraclough and Deacon were sold and a local lad called Tom Galley was signed from Cannock. Wolves had a run of poor results after the Christmas period and the frustration was evident in a violent home encounter against Chelsea in February. The referee had taken the unusual step of calling all outfield players from both teams into the centre circle and lecturing them about their conduct! The following month saw one of the greatest players the world has known make his debut as a professional player at Molineux. In beating Wolves by two goals to nil, Stoke City fielded Stanley Matthews for the very first time. His fierce shooting and clever wing play gave Wolves a very testing time.

At the start of their third season in the First Division a new face appeared among the players in the Molineux home dressing room. His name was Stan Cullis.

Little needs to be added to what has already been written and said about Stan Cullis. He was surely one of the greatest players and football managers Britain has ever produced. Of all Major Buckley's truly great footballer discoveries (men like Billy Wright and later John Charles), Cullis was the first and, for the Wolves, perhaps the most significant.

Born in Ellesmere Port of Wolverhampton parents, Stan Cullis was 'spotted' playing for a local team called Ellesmere Wednesday by Joe Foresaw. Foresaw, a Football Association referee, was a close associate of Major Buckley. Buckley invited the teenager to his home and interviewed him. The Major invited the young Cullis to join Wolves without even the formality of a trial. After he had signed, the Major told him after two months' training at the club that Cullis would make team captain in a very short time. However, by cutting short his summer break and assigning him duties as the groundsman's assistant, he ensured Cullis did not get ideas above his station. Cullis later wrote, 'my ego didn't last long with Major Buckley'. During his second season at Wolves, Cullis wanted a 10s a week pay rise. The Major flatly refused, whereupon Cullis left Molineux and was on his way back home before Buckley reluctantly agreed to the demand. It seems that, despite his position and harsh façade, Franklin Buckley didn't always get his way if his adversary stood up to him. He told Cullis he would have to earn his extra 10s, but as the young man became captain of Wolves at nineteen and England at twenty before managing Wolves as one of the most famous football clubs in the post-war world, it seems 10s a week well spent!

Stan Cullis came to admire Frank Buckley enormously and said that the Major 'was out of the top drawer'! The partnership that grew between the manager and his captain in the late 1930s became so strong and successful that their names became almost synonymous in a way reflected in the manager-captain relationship of Cullis and Billy Wright two decades later. Cullis moulded himself on the Major. His fitness and tough, uncompromising stance, as player and later as manager, brought Wolves the greatest period of glory they had ever known.

Cullis played three games at the heart of Wolves' defence during the 1934/35 season, sadly all defeats, and even though Wolves slipped to seventeenth in the League, a record Molineux attendance of 50,362 saw Sheffield Wednesday put the Molineux men out of the FA Cup in the fourth round.

Stan Cullis and the 'Buckley Babes', 1938.

Wolves' only goal was scored by Billy Hartill, who found the net 29 times during that season. It was to be Hartill's last year in Wolves' colours as he was sold to Everton at the end of the season. Hartill was one of seven players who left Wolves, and the exodus continued the following year. That season another nine left Molineux including the popular Dickie Rhodes and the Welsh international Dai Richards. Cecil Shaw, who had not missed a game in over five years, was transferred to local rivals West Bromwich Albion. Wolves finished the season back in fifteenth place, with Wrigglesworth having scored 12 goals, 'Boy' Martin 10 and Bryn Jones 9.

Although the 1935/36 season was fairly uneventful in terms of performances and results, it is remembered with sorrow by the Molineux faithful. In the December of 1935, Jimmy Utterson, a popular reserve goalkeeper, died from head injuries he had received in a game at Middlesbrough. Known for keeping up the morale of his fellow players by his fine ballad singing, or 'crooning', Utterson's loss was deeply felt by all at Wolverhampton Wanderers.

Rupert Street, Wolverhampton.

Despite this, a lot was happening in Franklin Buckley's personal life. His wife Madge had died in Birmingham some time earlier, and on Tuesday 23 June 1936 the Major remarried at Wolverhampton Registry Office. His new bride was Dorothy Isabelle Davis, the youngest daughter of a Wolverhampton couple. Dorothy's father, Thomas, was a brass founder, although the Wolves player Jimmy Dunn, who met her a number of times, believed she was also a one-time Major in the Women's Royal Army Corps. At thirty-one, she was over twenty years younger than Buckley, but there seems no doubt it was a happy marriage. The Wolves directors brought them a radiogram and the staff at Molineux clubbed together and gave the couple a toast rack to mark their happy day. After a honeymoon on the South Coast, the couple moved into a very stylish 'art deco' flat at St Judes Court on the Tettenhall Road. Frank Buckley had lived in a number of properties around Wolverhampton during his time at Wolves. Like Flat 4 at St Judes Court, all his homes in the town were within walking distance of Molineux. When he first arrived in Wolverhampton in 1927 he had weekday 'digs' in Whitmore Reans, while maintaining a home in Blackpool to which he returned each weekend. He later moved into a bungalow in Crowther Road, although he also had a very beautiful home at the hamlet of Island Pool, near Cookley on the A449. Built in 1791, the 'Old Cottage' was a typical English country cottage with low oak-beamed ceilings and leaded windows. During his years as manager of Wolves, Frank Buckley could always escape the pressures and stresses of the job by heading for this domestic idyll at Cookley. At the time of his marriage, Major Buckley was living in Rupert Street, at a house called 'The Nook'. Dorothy lived in a small red-brick semi-detached house at 13 Dunkley Street rather ostentatiously bearing the name 'Inglewood'.

Stanley Wilson was a teenager at the time of the outbreak of the Second World War. He was employed as an assistant at a grocery shop on the corner of Lime Street and Bristol Street in the Graisley area of Wolverhampton. The shop was owned and run by Dorothy's older brother, James Davies. Stan recalls the Major and Dorothy visiting the shop after home matches on Saturday afternoons in the early years of the Second World War. Buckley would playfully taunt his brother-in-law by saying, 'You had your faithful 5,000 before I came. Look at the crowds now!' Stan remembers the Major with kindness: 'He used to say to me and the other two shop boys, "Now be on standby! So many of my players have been called up I might have to play you at Molineux!"'

The season of 1936/37 was a watershed for Wolves, although it started very badly. Having won only 4 games out of 14, November 1936 witnessed Wolves languishing third from bottom of the First Division, although they did beat a visiting Yugoslavian team, Gradjanski, 4-2. After a 2-1 home defeat by Chelsea in front of the lowest home crowd for years (16,500)

St Jude's Court.

the crowd invaded the pitch from the South Bank and called for the resignation of Major Buckley and the board. Over 2,000 people were demonstrating in the hope of making the club management aware of popular anger over the spate of transfers. It was said at the time that Buckley had 'transferred a whole team' and although officials appealed for calm, it was to no avail. The crowd uprooted the goalposts before police reinforcements restored order. They offered Major Buckley an escort home, but being the old soldier and character that he was, he contemptuously refused this offer and walked home alone and unhindered. Amazingly, Wolves finished the season in fifth place, winning 17 of the games remaining after the debacle at the Chelsea match. The Wanderers also had a very good FA Cup run, reaching the sixth round for the first time in several years. Major Buckley later recalled the turnaround in club fortunes during the season in a letter to a close friend: 'I often think of the struggling days at "Wolves" when people wanted my head on a "charger" when I sold players in my policy of building.' At the end of the season, people were slapping him on the back. Such is the fickleness of football supporters.

The loyalty and support for their manager among Buckley's young players (who were to be called the 'Buckley Babes') was evident in the pre-season of 1937/38. Wolves had planned a close-season trip to Europe but they were forbidden to play on the Continent by the Football Association due to 'the numerous reports of misconduct by players of the Wolverhampton Wanderers Club during the past two seasons'. At their own behest, and unbeknown to the Major and the board, Cullis and his teammates wrote to the FA. They stated:

> We would like to state that far from advocating the rough play we are accused of, Major Buckley is constantly reminding us of the importance of playing good, clean and honest football, and we as a team consider you have been most unjust in administering this caution to our manager.

The Old Cottage, Island Pool.

Major Buckley and Dorothy, Christmas, 1947. (Mrs M. Powell and family collection)

Telling the powers that be at the FA what he thought of their actions could have cost Cullis any future chance of playing for his country and was not taken lightly. Considering that he was a young lad, barely out of his teens, it says much about his own integrity as well as his regard for the Major that he was willing to do this. However, the plain statistics bear out what Stan Cullis wrote. The Wolves of the Buckley era may have been competitive and physically tough, but in nearly eighteen years of him being manager at Molineux there were only seven sendings-off of Wolves players in all that time. The figures are even more remarkable when it is noted that four of these were accounted for by two players, Charlie Phillips and goalkeeper Alex Scott, each of whom was dismissed from the field of play twice.

The final two seasons before the outbreak of the Second World War were to be the finest in the whole history of Wolverhampton Wanderers up to that time. Although another ten players had moved on in the 1936/37 season, new names ever to be associated with Wolves' golden times appeared on the teamsheets.

Captained by Cullis and boasting players of great quality in Galley, Morris and Wolves' stalwart Joe Gardiner, the team was joined by the talented and prolific goalscorers Dickie Dorsett and Dennis Westcott. Alongside these was a sixteen-year-old North-Easterner whose 'twinkling feet dancing down the wing' were to thrill Wolves' followers for many years to come. This was Jimmy Mullen, who was joined in the ranks of old-gold and black by a slightly built Shropshire lad named William Ambrose Wright. Originally taken on as a forward, Buckley had almost lost one of the greatest football players in the history of the game when he threatened to send him home for being too small! After watching Billy Wright on the wing one day, the Major asked him to quickly manoeuvre from one foot to the other. Wright could not do this easily and was told by his manager to 'go to some dancing classes at the Civic Hall'. Although it may sound rather strange advice to give to a footballer, Billy Wright knew that Buckley was in effect suggesting a way for him to improve his balance.

However, like much surrounding Buckley's tenure at Molineux, this period of glory was surrounded in controversy. The use of monkey glands and pitch watering were both *causes célèbres* during this period, but it was the matter of one player's transfer that caused the Major and Wolves some problems.

At the start of the 1938/39 season, Buckley invoked the wrath of the Wolves fans by selling Bryn Jones to the Arsenal. This transfer, which was by far the most controversial of Frank Buckley's long career in football, was a rather protracted affair. Having served Wolves for almost five years, Bryn Jones played in 177 games and amassed 57 goals in that time. He was undoubtedly a jewel in Wolves' crown and their rise to prominence had coincided with his stay at the club. However, others cast envious eyes at him, wanting his superb skills for their own teams. Arsenal had become the nation's top club in the 1920s and 1930s under the legendary Herbert Chapman. In 1938 their boss, George Allison, was in desperate need of a forward to replace the famous Alex James, and even though a Wolves director called Oakley stated that 'Arsenal did not have enough money to buy Jones,' the Gunners made a bid of £10,000 for the little Welshman. While this was being considered Tottenham Hotspur came in with a counter-bid of £12,000 for Jones' services. The detail of the dealings got into the public domain and Jones, who seemed to have some reluctance in leaving Wolverhampton, took his time in deciding whether or not to agree to being transferred. One Wolverhampton resident remembers the drawn-out speculation surrounding the affair: '…it seemed to go on for ages. It was like electing the Pope!' Eventually, after Arsenal had increased their offer to a world-record fee of £14,000, Bryn Jones finally agreed to move to the north London club.

The move was very unpopular in Wolverhampton. Bob Sadler remembered his father's reaction when he read about Jones' move: 'Father flung the paper down in disgust! At a match the crowd invaded the pitch and pulled up the goal-posts. Father cheered them on!' The Major came in for a lot of criticism for the Bryn Jones transfer, and later recalled people spitting on the pavement behind him and his new wife as they walked around the town. In fairness it wasn't all Buckley's doing. Bryn Jones was his own man and one of the few at that time who was well able to stand up to the Major. He was a quiet man and disliked the public attention the transfer saga had heaped upon him. From the Major's point of view, the income of £14,000 from the sale was too good to miss out on. Major Buckley made some attempts to placate the fans by publicly stating 'the sky's our limit!' in the transfer market. He made a half-hearted attempt to sign Stanley Matthews from Stoke but this came to nothing.

However, as always, the Major had in mind a good replace-ment for the departed player. This was in the shape of Dickie Dorsett, who scored 26 goals in the 1938/39 season. Jones only played seventy-odd games for Arsenal and was never as prolific as he had been at Wolves. Stan Cullis believed that had war not have broken out and had he been brought back to Molineux, Jones's genius as a player could have been restored. Shortly after the transfer, Frank Buckley acquired a Welsh Terrier puppy, which somewhat perversely he named 'Bryn Jones'.

The team Buckley had assembled at the start of the 1937/38 season was one he intended to bring silverware to the trophy cabinet at Molineux. In that season they were runners-up in the League, gaining a total of 51 points and suffering only two home defeats. Although they were put out of the FA Cup by Arsenal in the fourth round, Wolves' League performances were very good indeed. For example, on 15 April 1938 they entertained Leicester City at Molineux. In a quite remarkable game, Wolves ran out winners by ten

goals to one, with Wescott and Dorsett scoring four goals
apiece. Wolves' goalie on the day, Welsh international Cyril
Sidlow, recalled that game over sixty years ago: 'They only
got one past me – and Cullis scored that!' Leicester's only
goal did indeed result from a collision between Wolves' captain and goalkeeper.

After all the fuss of the Bryn Jones transfer had died away,
Wolves started the 1938/39 season in good spirits. Although
they had only recorded two wins by the start of November,
this was followed by a run of eighteen games during which
they were only beaten once. With a great FA Cup run
that saw Buckley's young guns defeat teams like Bradford,
Liverpool, Everton and Leicester, there was a very strong
likelihood that Wolves would be the first team ever to win
the League and FA Cup double.

A 1930s caricature of Major Buckley.

The 'Nearly' team – the Wolves cup side of 1939.

However, it was not to be. Fully expected by most pundits to beat lowly Portsmouth in the Wembley final on Saturday 29 April, Major Buckley proudly led his team out onto the hallowed turf. This was the zenith of his achievements as a football manager. However, his young team 'froze' and, despite a fine goal from Dorsett, his team lost by four goals to one. Cyril Sidlow said that the Major left the team train at Birmingham when the Wolves returned home. At Wolverhampton station they were met by a handful of fans, although the streets around the town hall were thronged when the council later gave a civic reception for the team.

99

The Molineux men still had a chance of winning the First Division championship but, on 6 May, the final day of the season, they were unexpectedly held to a goal-less draw by Sunderland at Molineux. In effect, this was the last game Buckley's Babes would play, as war clouds were again gathering over Europe.

Major Buckley's Wolves had become the first team in the history of English football to be runners-up in the sport's two major competitions in the same year. They were within a hair's breadth of achieving the elusive 'double'. Had peace endured into the 1940s and Buckley kept his team together, there is little doubt they would have lifted a major trophy. But this is all conjecture.

A fully dedicated professional team of his choosing would not play for the Major again at Molineux. The nation had a greater need for the footballers of Britain. It needed them to change their club strips for khaki. After all, the late summer of 1939 was, in the Major's words, the time 'when Hitler had gone mad'.

SEVEN

AFTER THE DANCE

The 1938/39 was almost the most glorious in Wolves' long and distinguished history, but it was played out against a backdrop of unrest in Europe. Many had expected war to break out in 1938 when Hitler had invaded the Sudetenland, but the British Prime Minister Neville Chamberlain bought some time by signing the Munich agreement. Within weeks, as Hitler continued his intimidation of neighbouring countries, faith in Chamberlain's 'peace in our time' convictions had all but evaporated, and the word 'war' was on the lips of many. Even the Bryn Jones transfer saga had been seen as a 'healthy counterbalance to the perplexing problems of a harassed world'.

As the international crisis developed in the summer of 1939, Major Buckley advised his players to go along and join the Territorial Army in preparation for the anticipated call-up. With compulsory conscription having been introduced in Britain in 1916 after the slaughter of so many volunteer soldiers on the Somme, there would be no repeat of the controversy that had surrounded professional football at the outbreak of the First World War.

This would be 'total war' and the recent experience of the Spanish Civil War indicated that civilians in Britain would be subject to the same threats and dangers as front-line soldiers. Warfare technology had moved on a lot since Frank Buckley's experience of fighting in the trenches of the Western Front. Warplanes dominated the skies, and submarines patrolled the seas. Within months Britain was struggling for her very survival.

As soon as war was declared on Sunday 3 September 1939, the Football Association declared that the current season would be cancelled. The results of the three fixtures League teams had played would be struck from official records. As the declaration of war was made, the men of Molineux went into action. The board of directors offered to lend the government £5,000, interest free, towards the war effort and Frank Buckley gallantly tried to re-enlist into the Army for what would have been his third spell of service. However, considering his age (fifty-six years), he was perceived as being too old for active service, although his players started to receive their call-up papers almost at once. 'Boy' Martin, who had served with Wolves in the mid-1930s, joined the Ulster Rifles and Stan Cullis was conscripted into the Forces where he became a non-commissioned officer in the Army Physical Training Corps, where incidentally he served alongside Matt Busby of Manchester United fame. Billy Wright and Jimmy Mullen, who had both signed professional forms for Wolves in 1939, joined up. Like his teammate Cullis, Billy Wright became a physical training instructor. Both Wright and Mullen turned out for Leicester City during the war as 'guest' players. It was while with Leicester that they won their first silverware as footballers by helping Leicester win the Midland War Cup in 1941. In that competition they scored an impressive 23 goals between them.

Sadly, not all the players who had graced the Molineux turf and had responded to the nation's call were to return from active service. Joe Rooney, who had played in Wolves' midfield a couple of times in the final pre-war season, was to die in action at the age of twenty-four, and local lad Eric Robinson, one of the heroes of the 1942 War Cup win, drowned while on military training exercises shortly afterwards.

Even though all professional football competitions were suspended as soon as war was declared, within a few weeks a redesigned league system was introduced so that football could continue as a public morale booster. Initially, the government limited football crowds to 10,000 for safety reasons. The argument was made that civilian casualties would be high among football fans if German bombers attacked in daylight and grounds were hit. As the RAF rid the skies of German aircraft during the Battle of Britain this restriction was revoked. Wolves were initially designated as a member of the Football League South, although in subsequent war years they joined the Football League North. In the first disrupted wartime football season, Wolves won the Midland Regional League championship, having played against local Midland teams. Despite this success, the 1939/40 season cost Wolves very dearly and the club lost £17,700. Rather than face bankruptcy, it was decided that Wolves would close down for the 1940/41 season, thus allowing players like Billy Wright and Jimmy Mullen play for teams like Leicester City.

The famous Molineux ground was put to alternative use in the national interest during this time. The South Bank (which had originally been called the 'Hotel End'), was considered ideal for bulk storage and the Royal Navy kept large quantities of empty shell cases under tarpaulin sheets. An air raid shelter was constructed under the stand, the sign pointing to the location of which could still be seen right up until the building of the Jack Harris stand in the

1990s. Wolverhampton is blessed with having its football club ground closer to its centre than any other comparable town or city in England. Molineux has always been a focus of Wulfrunians' social activities other than football. During the hostilities large inter-faith prayer meetings took place at the ground and concerts were given by military bands for the entertainment of the people.

Despite not being allowed back into frontline forces, Franklin Buckley's military experience was not wasted. In 1940 he took command of a Home Guard unit.

The end of the 1939/40 season (albeit restricted), coincided with the fall of France. British Forces retreated to the coast and, in what was hailed as a miracle, thousands of troops were brought back home from the beaches of Dunkirk. Although safely back in Britain, the soldiers needed rest and reorganisation. Adding to the problems was the fact that the bulk of their equipment had been destroyed or left behind in the retreat to Dunkirk. The threat of a Nazi invasion was very high in the summer of 1940, and the Ministry of War quickly organised locally based military units to deal with any German invasion. Originally called the Local Defence Volunteers (LDV), these units were eventually known as the Home Guard. The Home Guard was made up of men engaged in essential 'reserve' occupations, such as working on the railways or in munitions factories, or men considered too old for the call-up, like Major Buckley. The Home Guard will always be associated (rather unfairly) in popular imagination with the 'Dad's Army' of television fame. The call to arms of such men during what was undoubtedly a time of national emergency did meet with some wry humour. Kathleen Quirke, a local factory worker at the time, remembers their establishment: 'The LDV? They were known as 'Look, Duck and Vanish.'

Despite early cynicism, the men in the Home Guard undertook their duties with pride. With no uniforms and only home-made weapons to start with, they patrolled the streets at night. They stood guard on facilities such as water-pumping stations and petrol tanks, both of which were considered vital to the war effort. Major Buckley held nightly meetings of the men in his unit in local church halls or in the local Territorial Army Hall. This was situated on the other side of Wolverhampton's West Park from his home at St Jude's Court. Being totally dedicated to individual physical fitness, Major Buckley would often march his men to the Molineux where they would use the club's exercising facilities and the pitch itself as a training ground.

After being closed down for a year, Wolves' management body (the Wolverhampton Wanderers Football Club Limited) declared a loss of £4,000. Although this was less than the deficit that would have been recorded had they played the 1940/41 season, it was felt safe and prudent to resume playing. Games were now very different affairs to what they had been before war had broken out. Buckley now had to field teams with any players he could muster. Footballers from other clubs who were then serving in local military bases, such as RAF Cosford, would be invited to play as 'guests'. Such men were popular with their fellow troops as they usually took several along with them to Molineux to cheer them on. Needless to say, they all got in free!

In the 1941/42 season matches were arranged on a 'back-to-back' basis, with Wolves playing the same opponents both home and away over the course of two weekends. Despite the difficulties, Wolves managed to play 37 games altogether and, thanks to the 'guest' system, fielded some fifty-four players over the course of the season. In each of the following two seasons Wolves called on the services of over sixty players. However, they weren't all 'outsiders' as many of Wolves' regular players turned out in the old-gold and black when they were on leave. Wright and Mullen both returned from Leicester and Dennis Wescott (who had 'guested' for Liverpool) also returned to the fold. Other

Wolves players were not to be so lucky. Alan Stein, who had been in the 1938/39 side as a sixteen-year-old, was captured by the Germans after a bombing raid.

The season was a very successful one, with Wolves lifting their first cup under Major Buckley's leadership. After progressing through a qualifying competition in which they met Buckley's old club Blackpool, Wolves beat both Manchester clubs and local rivals West Bromwich Albion in two-legged contests to meet Sunderland in the final of the War League Cup. Wartime conditions and conscription had seen match attendances drop as low as 4,000 but over 77,000 people saw Wolves and the Wearsiders' two-leg clash for the trophy. On 23 May Wolves drew 2–2 at Sunderland with Wescott bagging the brace. Wolves won the return leg 4–2 a week later, with Wescott again on the scoresheet. There was also a goal from Wolverhampton-born Jack Rowley, on loan from Manchester United.

Major Buckley with fourteen-year-old Cameron Buchanan at Molineux, 1940.

With this win under their belt, Major Buckley still tried to field quality teams, despite the difficulties. He adopted a policy of fielding very young players and was often heard to say, 'If he's good enough, he's old enough!' Indeed, it became commonplace for teenagers to turn out for Wolves on a regular basis. For example, Jimmy Mullen celebrated his seventeenth birthday in January 1940 by helping Wolves beat Coventry 3-0, and the average age of the Wolves team that faced Birmingham in March of that year was a mere nineteen years and six months, with wingers Billy Wright and Terry Springthorpe being only sixteen years of age. The following year, Buckley created a record by sending out a team to face Leicester with the average age of only seventeen years and one month. Quite a few eyebrows were raised in late September 1942 when a very young new face appeared on the right wing for Wolves. His name was Cameron Buchanan and at the age of fourteen years and fifty-seven days he was not only the youngest player to play first-team football for Wolves, but also probably the youngest to play at this level in a competitive match in the history of English football. Buchanan, who now lives in retirement in Dundee, remembers being watched by a Wolves scout while playing for Aulrie Academy in 1942. The scout was a colleague and friend of Buckley and Buchanan agreed to go with his father to visit the Major at his Wolverhampton home. Cameron readily admits that he had not heard of Wolverhampton, nor did he know where it was. He was willing to visit Wolves as they had the same team colours as his school side! He remembered that even young players had wartime duties to perform. He recalled one of his designated duties was 'fire-watching' from the roof of Fullwood's Tyres in Chapel Ash. Buckley tried to sign an even younger player called Menzies, but he was forbidden from doing this by the Football Association.

It was during the Major's war years at Molineux that Wolves were to have the first European player on their books. Emilo Aldecoa was a political refugee who had escaped the fighting of the Spanish Civil War in 1936. He turned out for Wolves as a left-winger between 1943 and 1945, appearing in Wolves' kit 48 times in all. In the first of his two seasons at Wolves, Aldecoa was the club's leading scorer and found the net 11 times. He remembered turning up at Molineux and Major Buckley not taking his eyes off him for a full fifteen minutes. He said the Major was 'a brilliant assessor of future players'.

In the two seasons between the War League Cup in 1941 and 1944, Wolves played another seventy-two games in the Football League North First and Second Divisions. Some of these games were qualifiers for the cup competition, but Wanderers' overall results were disappointing for the Major, as they won only 18 of these games and lost 40. This lack of consistency was hardly surprising given that Frank Buckley often did not know who he had available to send onto the field of play until shortly before a game. It was even reported that on more than one occasion an appeal had to be made to the crowd for one of their number to come forward to make up the numbers in the teams! Nonetheless, despite the problems, games always managed to go ahead and, for a couple of hours at least, the people of Wolverhampton could forget the worries and dreariness of the war and enjoy the entertainment and distraction that football at Molineux offered.

On Tuesday 8 February 1944 a bombshell hit the faithful of Wolves. Major Buckley requested that his contract be terminated. In other words he wished to resign!

This came completely out of the blue, especially as the fortunes of war had shifted in favour of the Allied nations. People could again envisage normal peacetime football, with Franklin Buckley leading a successful Wolverhampton Wanderers Football Club. The board of directors was as shocked as anybody by Major Buckley's decision, especially as the manager had agreed a ten-year contract with the club back in 1938. At that time it had been envisaged that he would stay as manager of Wolves until 1948, when he would be of an age to retire.

There has always been a great deal of speculation surrounding why Frank Buckley decided to leave Wolves when he did, and indeed why he wanted to leave at all. It was true that prior to coming to the club in 1927 he had moved from place to place both as a player and to some extent as a manager. But as he had been at Wolves almost two decades, achieving so much, many thought that he was settled and would stay for the duration of his contract. Some have said that the politics of the boardroom made him unsettled. With the impeding retirement of his chief supporter on the board, chairman Benjamin Matthews (Matthews had celebrated his seventieth birthday the week before and had made public his desire to step down from the board), he may have felt inclined to chance his arm elsewhere. Rumours at the time sinisterly connected the Major's decision to move on to the resignation of a local senior police officer and a black-market scandal. The murkiness of such tales makes their validity impossible to verify so they must remain mere speculation. There is nothing to suggest Major Buckley was involved in anything of this nature at all. A more simple reason for Frank Buckley's decision to go was that he saw no future challenge at Wolves and he was simply bored. He wanted a fresh challenge elsewhere. What is true is that Notts County, the oldest organised League club in England, came in and offered Frank Buckley £4,500 a year – a massive salary at the time – to take over their club and bring to it some of the success he had given Wolves. It was an offer too tempting to refuse. Notts County had tried to entice him away from Molineux in December 1943, but Buckley had refuted their overtures at that time, stating, 'I am not interested. I am under contract here.'

The true causes behind his decision to go were never made public and, despite speculation, Frank Buckley always maintained that he 'went for personal and private reasons'. So it was that on Tuesday 22 February 1944 the board of directors of Wolverhampton Wanderers issued a press statement declaring that it was 'with much reluctance and with very great regret to release Major Buckley from his engagement with the Club'. Private discussions (apparently harmonious and friendly) had taken place between the directors and Major Buckley. The only information made public stated that Buckley had given an assurance 'to do his utmost to further the interests of the Wolves and to take no action which would harm the club or its future prospects in any way whatsoever'. It finished by reassuring shareholders and supporters that a suitable successor would be appointed and the club would continue to prosper.

So it was that the link between the man and his team was broken. Writers have stated that 'Major Buckley and Wolves made each other famous.' His leaving Molineux is all the more difficult to comprehend given that he had stated uncategorically in 1938:

> Since coming to Wolverhampton ten years ago I have become so bitten by the Wanderers bug that no other club could ever interest me. It has been a pleasure to work in the town and, while we have had our differences, they have been plainly stated. I shall be happy to spend my football life with the club I so love.

But this was not to be and Buckley moved on.

The Notts County directors included a brewer called R.A. Shipstone, who had enough financial resources to fund Major Buckley's salary. The County board also had as one of its members a silk manufacturer called George Cottee. Cottee was a great admirer of Frank Buckley and pushed hard for his engagement at the Nottingham club. Also at the club was an old military colleague of Buckley's. This was a Major called Halford, who since the end of the First World War had turned his attentions to designing and developing aircraft. Buckley and his wife had a circle of friends in the Nottingham area, and so found the move across the English Midlands a fairly undisruptive experience. All the same, Frank Buckley did show some nostalgia for his old haunts, as it was noted that the first thing he did upon arriving at Meadow Lane was to hang a picture of the 'Old Cottage' at Island Pool upon his office wall, to remind him of the happy times he had spent there.

In his usual style, he had obtained a few good players for his new team, including Jackie Sewell, Bill Dickson and Paddy Radcliffe. The Major became a common figure at all the RAF and Army bases within a fifty-mile radius of Nottingham, where he watched inter-unit football matches on the lookout for raw talent. He would often arrive unannounced at a game in a borrowed car, having scrounged the petrol coupons that enabled his scouting mission to take place. In this way he 'spotted' the player who he considered to be his greatest 'find' for County. This was Jesse Pye, the son of a Treeton miner, who Notts County bought out of the Army so he could play for them.

However, despite a promising start, Frank Buckley was not to stay long at Notts County. Shipstone, the brewer and main backer of the Major, died, and Buckley felt somewhat vulnerable with the loss of this man's support. Despite the individual wealth of the fifteen directors, little money was made available for expenditure on the club. The Major later complained:

> I literally did not have a pair of boots in the dressing room nor the coupons to buy them with. The ground was bomb damaged and suffering from the wear-and-tear of war years, during which serious work on maintenance was impossible.

With such a high salary being paid to Major Buckley, a faction of the directors expected him to bring success to their club almost within weeks. They showed impatience and were not prepared for the sort of team-building programme Buckley had undertaken at Wolves, which had taken years to put in place. The Major became disillusioned and very unhappy. He even talked of leaving football altogether and buying a farm for him and Dorothy in the Worcestershire countryside. The situation was untenable and Franklin Buckley resigned. His last act as County's manager was to sell Jesse Pye to his old club, Wolves. 'He will pay back my salary and more besides,' Buckley is said to have commented as County made £10,000 out of the transfer.

Despite declaring the rather unrealistic desire for a farm, the Major stayed in football and, in a pattern almost reflecting his own playing days from before the First World War, Franklin Buckley now moved from managerial post to post, never staying at one club for any length of time. He was at Notts County for only a matter of months, but then was only out of work for a fortnight before he was approached to take on another club that needed his fabled magic touch. This club was Hull.

Major Buckley in his later years.

Hull City was a club that was described as being 'in the wilderness' at the end of the Second World War. It was a Third Division (North) outfit that, like Notts County, sought the success associated with the Major's spell at Wolves.

It was when he was at Molineux that the Major was asked for advice by a young Yorkshire master builder named Harold Needler who had a strong financial interest in Hull City. From this initial contact a strong friendship developed between the two men. Buckley's departure from Nottingham coincided with a revival in the Hull club, defunct throughout the Second World War. Harold Needler offered Frank Buckley the position of manager at Hull City and Buckley accepted, although his wage was a lot less than what he had received at Notts County.

In effect, the Hull City Buckley was taking on was a brand new club. It got into the Football League without the fierceness of an election purely because it acquired the legal rights and title of a pre-war club with the same name. A brand new pitch had been laid, although there were no stands. The new club had 'inherited' some items of kit ('a couple of sets of jerseys') and £1,500 in the bank. In a situation similar to that experienced by Wolves in 1923, a new company had been formed. The chairman was Harold Needler and with him on the board were his two brothers, George and John.

The parting of the ways between Buckley and Notts County came at the right time for the brothers and their associates who were in search of a manager. As they surveyed the emptiness of Boothferry Park, Harold Needler is reported to have said to the Major in an ironic fashion, 'I believe that you'll like this job.' Buckley was nonplussed and merely replied, 'It will mean starting from scratch, but I like a fight and I think I shall enjoy this one.'

The Major had barely twelve weeks to gather a team together. The club had to provide stands for spectators and changing facilities for players. Frank Buckley showed his old enthusiasm in the way in which he threw himself into the task of building a club up from the ground. 'I'm prepared to work twenty-four hours a day,' he said. Indeed, work on the new ground was going on almost twenty-four hours a day. Harold Needler and his brothers, who had a permit for £20,000 worth of buildings at the site of their ground, were busy on the stock exchange. They floated a public company with £50,000 capital and offered 140,000 shares at 5s each to raise £35,000 working capital. These were offered locally so that the citizens of Hull would have a feeling of part-ownership in their club. This was the first time a 'big' club had offered its potential supporters a financial stake in its prosperity. In order to drum up support for the venture, Major Buckley toured Hull addressing meetings almost as if he was a prospective Parliamentary candidate. In a few days, the club had received not only its £35,000 in share purchases, but also several thousand pounds in straightforward donations. As there were no large shareholders, Hull City became, in a sense, a 'co-operative', and a unique venture in football club management at the time.

Local workmen who had an interest in the new club succeeding put a great deal of enthusiasm into their work. It was said, 'they never slackened and when the five o'clock whistle went they took a swig of tea and went on working till nightfall. This was their club and they were working for it.' The public were welcome to drop in at the site and see how the work was progressing. One woman pushing a pram was interviewed at the ground. She was reported as saying, 'This is our club, you know, and we like to see it being born.' The main cantilever stand was built in six weeks. This stand would have erected even quicker had not a load of wires and tubes for reinforcing concrete gone missing on the railway for several days. The thousands of bricks that went into the stand and offices were all reclaimed from bombsites around Humberside and it was reported in the local press at the time that 'Every ounce of the ton of rubble that took shape as a huge Spion Kop behind the goal was a memorial to the blitz on Hull.'

In a sense Major Buckley had a clean drawing board on which to work, with a new stadium and a pitch greater in size than that at Wembley. With the superstructure of the Hull club in place, Buckley articulated his role in bringing success to the venture: 'The directors and public are so interested that the club can't fail so long as I can find the players.' And find them he did.

Over 26,000 turned out to see the first match at the new Boothferry Park. Despite the thunder and torrential rain Buckley had managed to get several good players to join the club. These included winger Ernest Bell, who had been a prisoner of war in Germany, and goalkeeper Billy Bly, who had distinguished himself in battles along the Rhine as the Allies pressed on into Hitler's Germany. He had also managed to sign a talented goal-taker named Jack Koffman from Manchester United, although as usual he sought young players from non-League football.

Buckley's 'old magic' did the trick and just one season and two months later Hull City were at the top of the Third Division (North) table. However, just as success was being reached and the Needlers' dream was being realised, a shadow was cast over the bright outlook at Boothferry Park.

The club was undoubtedly ambitious. At board meetings they spoke of their ambition to be in the First Division by 1951 and to build a 'super stand' to hold 20,000, giving Boothferry Park an overall spectator accommodation of 60,000 or more. But there were flies in the ointment that worked against these great ambitions.

Minor differences of opinion grew to the point where a breach was threatened between the Major and his board. Not for the first time in his career, the rate at which the Major wished the club to develop was unpopular with the men holding the purse strings, namely the directors. Leeds United were aware of the schism developing at Hull. They were prepared to offer Frank Buckley a considerable wage increase to come and manage the 'Lilywhites' at Elland Road. Despite a short-lived reconciliation between the board and their manager, Frank Buckley did move on to Leeds in April 1948. He left Hull in a good position and in football terms truly put the club on the map. Under Buckley they had finished eleventh in the Third Division (North) in 1946/47 with 40 points, and the following season he left them in fifth position with 47 points. In 1948/49 they gained promotion to the Second Division by being crowned champions of the Third. Hull City were able to achieve this accolade mainly because of the players Major Buckley had brought into the side while he was manager at Boothferry Park.

The Leeds United that Buckley took on at the end of the 1948 season was yet another football club in the grip of crisis. Leeds had opened their gates to First Division football at the end of the Second World War but did not survive long in the top flight. At the end of the previous season Leeds had finished in last place in the First Division, with a miserly 18 points and having lost 30 of their 42 fixtures. Having being relegated to the Second Division, there was no quick turnaround in the 1947/48 season. In fact the decline continued, and the club finished well down in the lower division, finally ending up in eighteenth place. With finances draining away and little sign of improvement on the horizon, something had to be done.

A well-heeled haulier named Sam Bolton had taken over as chairman of the Leeds board of directors. It was at his behest that the Major was approached and subsequently appointed. However, Buckley's appointment as the manager of Leeds did not meet with universal approval. The debacle at Notts County was still fresh in the minds of many and Frank Buckley was by this time sixty-four years of age – almost a pensioner in post-war Britain. Nonetheless, Buckley was undoubtedly a man for a crisis, and he fully realised his priorities when he took over the hotseat at Leeds.

He knew he had to halt the club's decline and rebuild the team with little or no financial resources. He started with a clearout of players, and the Major was not afraid to court unpopularity by getting rid of some popular men. Aubrey Powell was such a player. Having been given a verbal lashing by Buckley, he found himself transferred to Everton for £10,000 a month after Buckley's arrival. The Major bought in new players such as the Scottish international full-back Jimmy Dunn and a wing half called Tommy Burden that Buckley had had on the books at Wolves. Along with a forward called Browning, who was a regular rather than a prolific goalscorer, Buckley established a team that managed to arrest the club's slide. At the end of his first full season at Leeds, 1948/49, they finished in fifteenth place in the Second Division, but the following campaign saw a great improvement in their fortunes. In the 1949/50 season Leeds went up to fifth place in the table and also experienced their best ever FA Cup run. Under Buckley, they got as far as the quarter-finals where in front of a crowd of 62,000 they were finally beaten by the odd goal by Arsenal. Buckley's 'touch' was working again and it seemed only a matter of a short time before Leeds would be promoted back to the top flight. However, it was not to be under Franklin Buckley's leadership.

The season that marked the century's halfway point again witnessed Leeds finishing fifth in the Second Division. Most fans would remember 1949/50 as the season that Frank Buckley discovered a youth who was to become arguably Leeds' greatest player – the legendary John Charles. Known as the 'Gentle Giant', John Charles was to win 24 international caps for Wales. He started his football career on the ground staff at Swansea Town (later City) FC. Charles could play at either centre forward or centre half and was a prolific goalscorer. He was the first Home Countries player to be transferred to a continental side in 1957 when he joined Juventus for a record fee of £65,000. While in Italy he won three championship medals and was Italy's Footballer of the Year. John Charles had a second spell with Leeds in the 1960s before returning to Italy and finishing his playing career with Roma.

Recommended by Alf Pickard, one of his scouting associates based in South Wales, Buckley described how he had first seen John Charles:

> I shall never forget that morning when I first met John Charles. I was sitting in my office when they bought in a giant of a boy. He told me he was fifteen. He stood 6ft and weighed more than 11st. He wanted a trial at my club as centre half. I thought 'They don't come that big very often: it may be too good to be true.'

It wasn't. Within ten minutes of watching him play, Major Buckley knew he had a world-beater. Buckley had signed the boy even before he had time to shower! The Major always described John Charles as 'the best I've ever seen'.

However, despite the acquisition of such a fine player and again finishing a respectable fifth in the table, Buckley could take Leeds United no further. At the end of the following season, 1951/52, Leeds finished sixth and, although they had a good cup run, promotion seemed as far away as ever. In the summer of 1953, Leeds had slipped to mid-table (tenth) and at the age of seventy manager Frank Buckley resigned, realising he could do no more for the club with so little available to spend on new players.

Staggering as it might seem, Franklin Buckley at the age of seventy was not yet finished in football management! He had one last roll of the dice. Upon leaving Leeds, he and Dorothy returned to the West Midlands and Frank Buckley was approached by the directors of Walsall to take over the Fellows Park club. He readily agreed to become the thirteenth manager in the club's history. The announcement of his appointment was made to a packed meeting of the club's supporters at Walsall Town Hall in July 1953. The folk memories of what he had achieved 'down the road' at Wolverhampton, a club in a similar state to Walsall, were strong, and despite his later under-par performances as a football manager, hopes were high that Frank Buckley, 'the 'Molineux magician', could become the 'Walsall wonder'. There were scenes of wild jubilation when he declared to the assembled throng, 'This may be my last job in football, but it will be my best!'

Walsall FC, or the 'Saddlers' as they were nicknamed, were a decent enough club. However they always seemed to be overshadowed by their more successful neighbours, namely Wolves, Albion, Birmingham City and Aston Villa. Walsall had all the features of a club that Buckley might have brought some success to. It was languishing at the wrong end of the Third Division (North) and there was not a lot of money to spend on new players. The season that Buckley arrived Walsall had finished twenty-fourth in the division. He managed to bring in players with experience of performing at higher levels, but he was unable to make much impact in just over two years at Fellows Park. Despite attracting bigger crowds and increasing the squad size by twenty per cent, the Saddlers stayed in twenty-fourth place at the end of the Major's first season in charge. The club had to apply for re-election to the League. It was widely believed that sufficient supporting votes were secured mainly because of other clubs' regard for Major Buckley's personal reputation and standing in the game.

During his second season in charge at Walsall results improved little and both directors and fans began to realise that Major Buckley's fabled skills of football management were failing. Few new players arrived. His attempts to find raw footballing talent, which might be developed, from the mines and factories failed dismally. His scouting network, so long the mainstay of his talent spotting, was breaking up as his scouts became old and retired. Complaints about the team's poor performances appeared in the local press all through the spring of 1955 and a group of disgruntled supporters started barracking the Major at every home game. Lampooned by local cartoonists as the 'Gurroles' (from 'Good old' as in 'Good old Walsall'), this group became very vociferous and the message of discontent they were sending out was not lost on the Walsall directors.

Attempts were made to support Major Buckley in his role of manager. On 17 June 1955, Jack Love, a one-time successful inside forward with Nottingham Forest, was appointed assistant manager at the club. His specific brief was 'to intensify the search for young players'. Love, a Scot and the first holder of the post of assistant manager at Fellows Park, was highly regarded among the people of Walsall. He was a hero of the Second World War, having won the Distinguished Flying Cross for the bravery he had shown as an RAF officer during the Allies' crossing of the Rhine in the spring of 1944. Oddly enough, Jack Love carried war wounds similar to Major Buckley's, for he too had been hit by shrapnel during his active service.

Despite Love's appointment, Walsall finished the season poorly and ended up only one place higher than the previous year. Nevertheless a mood of optimism was evident for the forthcoming 1955/56 season, especially as a new coach, Eric Jones, was appointed and successful attempts were made to raise funds from the public to finance the purchase of new players.

Despite the optimism the season started terribly. By the beginning of September, Buckley's team had played five games and had managed only two draws. The writing was on the wall for Frank Buckley.

Walsall's sixth game was against Newport at Fellows Park on 3 September 1955. With only a minute to go the Saddlers were leading by three goals to two. With almost the final kick of the game, lowly Newport equalised, leaving many fans with an 'exasperated reflection on what might have been'. It was the last straw! The majority of the 14,500 crowd realised this would be Frank Buckley's last game in charge of Walsall. Maybe fewer realised they had just witnessed his swansong in the professional game.

On the following Tuesday, a meeting took place between the Walsall directors and Frank Buckley. After proceedings had finished, the chairman, J.N. Longmore, confirmed that Major Buckley's contract, due for renewal the following March, had been terminated 'by mutual consent'. He added rather vaguely, 'We have differed on a matter of policy – that's all I can say!' Major Buckley, described as being 'stern faced', simply said, 'I have no statement to make.'

Although he later said he had offers from other clubs, Major Buckley had finished with professional football, almost fifty years to the day after he played his first professional game. At the age of seventy-three, Franklin Charles Buckley had reached the end of the road in football. The pathos of the situation in the final days was summed up by Eddie Holding. Eddie, a Wolverhampton-born lad, was playing for the Major at the time. Eddie witnessed Major Buckley coming into the home dressing room after a rather poor result by the Walsall team at the start of the 1955/56 season. A group of players were involved in some horseplay in the baths and Buckley complained that it was about time they concentrated on winning matches. Alan Grubb, a former Tottenham Hotspur player, shouted across the changing room, 'What's up Buck?' The Major simply turned away.

No one would have dared speak to Major Buckley in such a manner at the height of his powers. Even those who did not fear him and were able to stand their ground would have shown more respect. But this was a different age – a different world. Men had come back from the Second World War and the social order had changed. Titles and experience did not hold the same sway as they had before. A new age was dawning. Football was to become more than a mere

The Major's last home, at Mellish Road, Walsall.

game and players were to reach an almost godlike status in the eyes of the public. Frank Buckley had done much to bring that about, but now his day was over.

Frank Buckley left Walsall FC and football management for good. He and Dorothy continued to live in the town. For the remainder of his life, Major Buckley lived quietly in a stylish flat at 24 Mellish Road on the eastern side of the town, writing the occasional newspaper article and giving interviews. Despite the good earnings he had made earlier in his career, the couple were not well off and seemed to have suffered some financial hardship at times. Frank Buckley's health declined slowly over the next decade and he suffered badly from bronchial problems, heart trouble and failing eyesight.

Major Buckley passed away on 22 December 1964 at the age of eighty-two. His death was due to heart failure. His funeral service took place at SS Mary and John's RC Church in Wolverhampton, the town to which he had brought so much fame. It is said his ashes were scattered on the Malvern Hills – a place he loved greatly.

EIGHT

IN THE LAND OF THE GIANTS

There is an old Irish saying that some men seem tall because they stand on the shoulders of giants. It is undoubtedly true that many gained their reputations through what they had learnt from Major Buckley. He was truly a giant of English football before the Second World War. In order to fully appreciate his place in the history of the national game, it is important to compare his approach, methods and philosophy on football with those of his contemporaries – other football managers of his era.

Many football historians agree that the greatest pre-war football club manager was Herbert Chapman, who gained his greatest fame while managing Arsenal between 1924 and his untimely death in 1935. Major Buckley is often mentioned alongside Herbert Chapman as the greatest of their day, although their approach and achievements in football were very different.

Herbert Chapman, like Buckley, hailed from the North of England. He was born in Kiveton in South Yorkshire in 1873, but he had a far less exalted playing career than the Major. Chapman's greatest claim to fame as a player was when he turned out for Tottenham Hotspur's reserves. Even then he was best remembered for his lemon yellow boots rather than his playing ability. At the age of thirty-four, he had his first taste of football management when he took over as player-manager at Northampton Town in the Southern League.

A number of commentators have made the point that it isn't always the case that great players make great managers. The skills needed in organising and perceiving the game on and off the field vary greatly. Football history is littered with cases of highly acclaimed players subsequently failing as managers. The skill of seeing the wider picture as opposed to having to concentrate on individual personal perform-ance means that not everyone is suited to management. As one former England international wrote in the 1970s after a particularly fraught spell as a manager in the Football League, 'One minute you are walking off the pitch, the next you are having to manage fifty people.' A good example of this phenomenon was when Billy Wright, then England's most capped footballer, retired from playing, and took over the reins at Arsenal. In the four years he was in charge at Highbury, the Gunners failed to win anything, although, in fairness, Wright has been credited with assembling the squad that won the double in 1971.

So it was that Chapman, although not a great player in his own right, had early success in management. By the end of his second season in charge, he had led Northampton to the Southern League championship. In 1912, he moved to Leeds City, a much bigger club. He narrowly failed to secure Leeds City promotion to the top flight on the eve of the First World War. He then left football for a while during the wartime shutdown. During this time he ran a munitions factory, which proved useful experience in gaining manage-rial skills outside of football.

Upon resuming his management role at Leeds when peace was declared in 1918, Chapman was involved in a scandal that led to the Leeds club's suspension by the FA for illegal payments to players. Chapman himself was suspended for a year for being involved in burning the club's books before they could be scrutinised by the FA. During this period he took a partnership in an engineering firm, although he was tempted back to football management in 1920. In that year he was invited to take over at Huddersfield Town. This was the same year that Major Buckley was having his first taste of running a team at Norwich, but Chapman was far more successful. Within two years Town had won the FA Cup and by 1924 had secured the League Championship by goal difference over Cardiff. Huddersfield went on to hold the title for the two successive seasons with the team that Chapman had built. However, Chapman left to manage Arsenal at the end of the 1923/24 season.

Despite a slow start to his regime at Highbury, by the 1930s Chapman was to bring Arsenal great success. In 1930, they would win the FA Cup – the first trophy in their history secured by a 2-0 win over Huddersfield. The following year they were to become the first London club to be crowned League champions, with a points total that was not to be beaten for three decades. They were to remain champions for three seasons (1933-1935) – a feat not to be repeated until the Premiership era. But all that was for the future.

In 1924, having being 'headhunted' by the Gunners' chairman, Henry Norris (who had tried to secure Frank Buckley's service just a few years earlier), Chapman came to Highbury at a time of change in the national game. He demanded, and was given, far more free rein in managing his team than many of his counterparts. Unlike any others at the time he devised an overall strategy involving far more than just picking a team from the players the directors had chosen to buy. He was the right man at the right time. With a proven successful management record at lower levels, the time was right for him to put his ideas into practice.

An alteration in the offside rule, which reduced the number of opposition players who had to be between the attacking forward and the goal, opened up matches and allowed far more goals to be scored. Chapman accommodated this by changing his team's formation to bring in a third central defender, or 'stopper' as he was termed. Thus, the Gunners would be better able to absorb and nullify attacks, and rely on wingers to come in more centrally to shoot at goal. This tended to make his team very defensive, and he bought players with specific attributes to fit into his team strategy, whereas Frank Buckley believed in individual fitness and constant fast attacks on the opponents' defences. In fact, in the 1931/32 season, when Wolves were heading for promotion, the London press took exception to Wolves' style of play in comparison to Arsenal's. They sneeringly referred to Buckley's tactics as 'unscientific' and accused Wolves of using 'extreme vigour' in their primitive 'kick and rush' playing style. Wolves hit back and dismissed these condemnations. 'Let London notice,' one critic wrote, 'that Wolves do not run a third back. That is why the first team have got 110 goals and the reserves 118.' Herbert Chapman encouraged players to think in terms of 'playing zones', where they would be responsible for achieving their part in the team's overall game plan. The Major however wanted his men to be flexible in their approach, and interchangeable in their playing roles. On the field of play, Herbert Chapman's Gunners made far more use of set pieces such as free-kicks and corner kicks as a means of gaining a strategic advantage during the course of a match. A lot of teams had not practised routines on how to make the most of the advantage a set piece might provide.

Chapman and Buckley concurred on a great deal, including the idea of numbering player's shirts, and also keeping influential outsiders away from the team while they were at the stadium, but it was in the nature of the relationship they had with their players where the greatest difference between the two men could be seen. Herbert Chapman knew that when he acquired a player, he was getting more than a fit man who was good at kicking a ball or saving a shot. He knew that his men had their own ideas and expertise gained from years of playing that represented a valuable resource and should not be wasted. He organised planning meetings with all his players prior to each fixture. Usually taking place on Friday lunchtime at a local hotel, at these get-togethers his players would be encouraged to exchange ideas and knowledge of their forthcoming opponents. A 'match plan' for the forthcoming game would eventually evolve, with each player having a pretty detailed idea of his role in the overall plan. This involvement and what now might be termed 'shared ownership' of the planned strategy was a practical way of acknowledging the players' professionalism, worth and value to the team. It was evident in the approach of other football managers of the period such as Bob Hewison of Bristol City, Harry Curtis of Brentford, Tom McIntosh of Tranmere Rovers and Jimmy Seed at Charlton Athletic. Such involvement with players would not suit Major Buckley's management style, although John Charles related that Buckley stood his players a drink at the end of a season. His inclination and experience of managing men in the military made his approach far more directive. This is not to say that Major Buckley didn't consult with others. Stan Cullis recalled that, as Wolves' skipper, he had regular post-match meetings with the Major. These usually took place on the Monday morning following a game where the team as a whole, as well as individual performances, were discussed and analysed. Elements of a military model of communication and planning can be seen in this practice. It is as if Frank Buckley, the commander and sole strategist, was liaising with his junior, middle-ranking subordinate, but that's as far as it would go. Frank Buckley would never meet his players in the same way Chapman had. He needed to be perceived as the biggest personality at the club if his authority was to be maintained and not questioned. This is underlined from his time at Leeds when he told the former RAF pilot, Ken Chisholm, who was a good striker and popular personality, 'This city's not big enough for both of us and I'm not going.' Within weeks, Chisholm had been exchanged for the Leicester City player Ray Iggleden.

Although he was far from being a 'soft touch', Chapman believed he could get the best out of his players by being approachable and receptive. 'He must share their troubles, help them out of difficulties, and within the limits of discipline, be their pal,' he wrote. This was an anathema to Major Buckley who, although capable of acts of individual kindness, would never jeopardise his status by becoming a player's 'pal'. He was not alone in this at the time. Harry Storer of Coventry City was similar to the Major in his approach to players, and both men saw the dressing-room as basically a barracks where constant monitoring was needed to weed out skivers and sissies. Like Buckley, Storer often used sarcasm to berate his players. Storer, cited as the inspirational role model of both Brian Clough and Peter Taylor, once laid into a player after the end of a match for his poor performance. The startled man defended himself by stating that he had not actually played in the game. 'Well,' said Storer, 'if you can't get into this team, you *must* be useless!' Storer was noted for countering the perennial question from players, 'Boss, why am I in the second team?' with the retort, 'Because we don't have a f——ing third team!' Frank Buckley and Harry Storer were managerial soul mates.

Another big difference between the two managers was that Herbert Chapman was able to buy the players best suited for his strategic game, whereas Buckley made his name by developing raw talent and selling it on. For example, as soon as he arrived at Arsenal, Herbert Chapman was able to purchase a big, scheming inside forward called Charlie Buchan who he considered central to his plans. Described as 'too clever to play for England', Buchan was signed from Sunderland for an initial £2,000, with an added £100 per goal he scored. The chairman of the club, Henry Norris, was suspended by the FA for allegedly offering illegal inducements to gain the player's signature. Even so, Major Buckley did on occasion get the chequebook out for a good player (for example he signed Wilf Lowton from Exeter in 1929 for £1,400. After turning out more than 200 times in old-gold and black, Lowton returned to City in 1935). However, this was exceptional as he prided himself on finding and developing raw talent costing very little or nothing at all. Herbert Chapman was fortunate to have large financial resources to call upon, and it was not for nothing that the Arsenal of the 1920s and 1930s were called 'the Bank of England club'. Other major signings, such as Ted Drake, Cliff Bastin and Alex James, followed Buchan to Highbury and the most powerful and successful team in England was gradually built up. And it showed.

Buckley's Wolves and Chapman's Gunners met on 9 occasions when the two men were managing their respective teams (1927-1936). Wolves won only 1 of these fixtures, although they drew twice. However, at two of these games Arsenal put a massive seven goals past Wolves. It is little wonder that the papers of the time referred to Arsenal as Wolves' 'bogey team'.

It might be easy to run away with the idea that pre-war football managers on the whole tended to include hard men and objective tacticians, and that any humour associated with the sport was at best cutting and more usually vitriolic. But that was not always the case. Although Major Buckley may have been exhibiting an attitude of whimsy when he took on a second-string goalkeeper called Charlie Chaplin in the 1930s, a more natural comic and colourful character was to be found in the manager of the Portsmouth team Wolves met in the FA Cup final of 1939. Like Buckley, Pompey's manager Jack Tinn knew the value of publicity.

Jack Tinn had been appointed Portsmouth manager in 1927, the same year Frank Buckley had arrived at Molineux. In that year his team had gained promotion to the top flight on goal average, by a mere 1/200 of a goal. He had bought his club success, and the people loved him. He was a real character. Tinn wore a large overcoat with 'stolen from Bud Flanagan' written on the label. He was known for wearing 'lucky' shoe coverings, commonly called 'spats'. Publicity photographs of Freddie Worrall fastening his manager's spats appeared in the national press in the late 1930s, and it was not long before Tinn had earned the nickname 'Jack Spatt'. He was liked for his sense of humour and he used the psychology of humour to relax his players before a big game. He often employed a music hall comedian to crack jokes to get the players in a good frame of mind before going out onto the park. His understanding of human behaviour was best seen just before the start of the 1939 final. Autograph books were circulated among the teams prior to kick-off. The Portsmouth players got the books after the Wolves had signed them. Jack Tinn delightedly pointed out to his players that the Wolves' signatures were shaky and ill-formed. They showed all the signs of the Wolves' nervousness. He confidently told his excited players, 'You've got them!' And they had. Against all expectations, Wolves lost 4-1 and were said to have 'frozen' on the day. Perhaps their jitters about the big occasion coupled with their fear of displeasing the Major made them perform well below par. Perhaps Major Buckley's authoritarianism wasn't always the best way to get the most out of footballers.

So, there were other approaches to football management besides the Major's. Whenever this period is considered, the comparison between him and Herbert Chapman always comes to the fore and the two men are judged as the managerial 'giants' of their day. Buckley, like Chapman, has been rightly described as 'progressive'. The two men represented a new breed of football administrator in those far-off pre-war days of English football. Both were visionaries and both had ideas well ahead of their time. However, whereas Chapman was the corporate tactical planner, the Major's ideas revolved more around how the sport would be organised and administered in the future, and how the physique of individual players might be enhanced and developed. Both Buckley and Chapman can claim credit for being the first of the modern football managers. They were more than club directors' lackeys. They freed themselves and others in their wake from onerous club administration in favour of focusing on what was happening on the pitch. They were the 'new men' who acquired squads and picked teams; who managed money and resources; who talked to the press. They became the men seen as synonymous with their club – the public face. For the first time in football history such managers became as famous as the players who turned out for them.

Buckley was open to new ideas, but rigid in his attitudes towards players. This inflexibility did not stand the test of time. Chapman died before his ideas and practices could become outdated, and he is now recalled in the golden glow stemming from his great success and achievements at Arsenal. Frank Buckley's chances of lifting silverware were always going to be more difficult. They were effectively put paid to by the onset of the Second World War. Although he carried on in management for another decade and a half after his finest season of 1938/39, in the end he became an anachronism – a dinosaur that was locked in the past.

Football was to move on. He wasn't able to.

NINE

IN THE LABORATORY OF SOME MAD PROFESSOR

So why was Major Frank Buckley considered one of the greatest football managers in the country all those years ago?

No doubt Buckley was influential on how football developed, but he was not particularly successful in terms of cups or titles that his teams won. In fact, for a man who had managed no less than seven professional clubs and who in later life boasted of his 'fifty years in football', his record appears poor if judged solely on the trophies collected over the years.

However, there was a great deal more to Frank Buckley than that. As football management is a complex and difficult occupation, it is best to look at the different aspects involved, so that an appreciation of Major Buckley's huge contribution to football in the twentieth century may be gained.

When it comes to the way in which he managed the greatest assets any football club has, namely its players, Buckley was quite unequivocal. Although he mixed with one or two players away from football on the golf course, he never became 'pals' with the men who played for him as some managers did. This allowed him to be fully objective about the composition of his teams, but led some players to become quite shocked when they realised the relationship they believed they had with him was perceived differently in the Major's eyes. For example a number of former Buckley players found that they had been put on the transfer list without prior warning. They may have thought that they were doing 'okay' for the Major but this would not stop him moving players on from the club. He had no 'favourites' in a personal sense, but there were players he grew to trust for their leadership qualities on the field of play; something more akin to a partnership developed with these men. The Major's relationship with Stan Cullis as Wolves' captain was a good example of this.

Much of Buckley's attitude towards his players was based on his experience as an Army officer. This worked well until the Second World War led people to question established social hierarchies. It was not for nothing that he retained his wartime title of 'Major'. This brought him immediate social status in the Britain of the 1920s and 1930s. It was a useful weapon in his armoury when it came to managing and directing others. Buckley was aware of the status this gave him and to some extent tried to reinforce it. He maintained a style of dress that was incongruous with the industrial surroundings of the clubs he managed. The flat cap, 'plus four' trousers, long socks and brogue shoes were more in keeping with the dress of a country squire. As the years progressed it made him seem a little eccentric. Not that that would have worried Frank Buckley. He was a unique character and his trademark style of dress ensured that everyone knew he was a 'one-off' and his own man. This image that he created stuck in the minds of people who saw him. Speaking over sixty years later, Don Bilton, who was a young goalkeeper on Wolves' books in Buckley's era, recalled the Major as 'a big red-faced man, dressed like a member of the gentry, striding through the streets of Wolverhampton on his way to Molineux, accompanied by a pack of four dogs'. When managing Leeds United in the post-war years he was remembered in much the same manner. Tommy Burden recalled: 'He wore Oxford Bags and his shoes were hand-welted, shining to perfection. You didn't call him "Frank", you called him "the Major".' Major Buckley had high standards of personal behaviour and manners, and expected to see the same in others. Burden continued his reminiscences of Major Buckley: 'He spoke like an upper-class gentleman. I remember him bawling out Len Browning one day for not saying "good morning"!'

There were other aspects of his managerial approach that stemmed from his military background. He was well known to have been a strict, some might say harsh, disciplinarian. A number of players, especially younger ones, were really frightened of him. Billy Wright wrote of hiding in the boiler room when he heard the steel-capped toes of the Major's brogue shoes echoing on the marble floors of Molineux. It took a lot of courage for a young lad still in his teens to face Major Buckley without trepidation. Jack Charlton, the backbone of England's successful 1966 World Cup team recounted an encounter he had with the Major when he was a trainee on the ground staff at Elland Road:

> Unlike the pros, we just got two weeks' holidays in the summer, and while they were away, our job was to remove the weeds from the pitch and replace them with grass seed. I remember being sat out there one day with Keith Ripley, another ground staff boy. We must have looked pretty forlorn, the two of us, and to gee us up he said he'd give us five shillings with every bucket we filled with weeds. Now that was an offer we couldn't refuse.

By the time we were finished, we had filled six buckets, and cheeky bugger that I was, I marched straight up to the Major's office. And when he asked what I wanted, I told him I was there to claim my thirty bob for the weeds. He nearly blew a bloody gasket! 'Get out of here!' he bellowed. 'You're already getting paid to do that work – don't ever let me see you up here again with your buckets.'

Jimmy Dunn, a Liverpudlian, who became a great star of the Wolves side of the 'Golden Fifties', recalled playing as a youngster at wartime Molineux:

I was only seventeen at the time. I worked as a fireman on the railways during the week and played for Wolves at weekends. In one game I tried really hard and ran my heart out. The ball hit me in the crotch. I was in agony and had to be stretchered off. While the physio had me on the treatment table and was administering an ice pack, Buckley stormed in and pushed his face right into mine. 'You deserved that,' he said and stormed out. The physio told me to go to the lavatory and try to pass water. While I was doing this, Major Buckley came in and ordered me back onto the pitch. I really had been trying my best.

Not all youngsters had such a rough time from the Major. Cameron Buchanan recalled coming to Wolverhampton as a fourteen-year-old with his father to meet the Major:

The promises he made were unbelievable. I always liked him, and thought he had an open, honest face. If you accepted the discipline from him, it made you feel better. He was way ahead of his time.

Cameron also described a paternalistic Frank Buckley who may not have been recognised by those who saw him only as a disciplinarian. A youth had come up from the Welsh valleys in the hope of impressing Major Buckley in a trial match. Having been through a severe economic slump in the 1930s, money was still very tight in the Rhondda. The lad's family had kitted him out with the best clothing they could lay their hands on for his trip to Molineux. Although meticulously washed and cleaned, much of the boy's outfit simply didn't fit him well at all. Cameron remembered the boy was very big for his age and the clothing was tight. After the trial game, Major Buckley took the boy into Wolverhampton and from his own pocket bought him a whole new outfit of clothes to return home to South Wales with. Jack Charlton, despite his run-in with the Major over the weeds incident, knew there was a generous side to him. He recalled something similar when Frank Buckley was at Leeds. Upon seeing young Jack's badly worn shoes one day, the Major asked him if they were the only ones he had. The young player replied that they were. The following day Major Buckley gave young Jack Charlton 'a pair of Irish brogues, the strongest, most beautiful shoes I had ever seen. And I had them for years.' Charlton recently said that he still has them to this day!

The military approach also made Major Buckley a stickler for detail when it came to dealing with his players. Eddie Holding recalled his father telling him of an incident concerning a Wolves player called Dickie Rhodes who was seen coming out of the Chillington Working Men's Club in the Willenhall Road area late one Thursday night in the late 1920s or early 1930s. It was commonly known that the Major applied an early evening curfew to his players two days prior to a match so they would get plenty of sleep and rest. A sneaky member of the public, who might even have been in the pay of Buckley, contacted the Major about seeing Rhodes leaving the club. The following day Buckley confronted Rhodes over this breach of discipline and dropped him from the weekend trip away to play Bury. Rhodes asked if he could go on the team coach and watch the game, but Buckley refused. A determined Dickie Rhodes travelled all the way to the Lancashire club in a friend's motorbike sidecar. When he tried to get in using the usual practice of presenting his FA card as a pass,

Major Buckley was waiting for him and sent him packing. It seems there was no getting one over on the Major!

Frank Buckley knew the personal fitness of players was key to getting results on the park. As a non-smoker and very occasional drinker himself, Buckley expected his players to be moderate in their vices. He advised young players not to smoke and it must be remembered this was well before the days when medical researchers had discovered the harmful effects of tobacco. Eddie Holding wrote to Major Buckley in 1945 when he had taken over at Notts County. In the reply he received from the Major he was advised to 'Get all the outdoor exercise you can, and plenty of sleep and do *not* smoke!' He also reassured Eddie that he would give him a trial later in the year: 'You have my word, never fear'.

Buckley's behaviour codes and expectations of his players were contained in a small yellow-covered pocket book he had printed. Apart from the specific instruction and advice he gave players on diet, notes on work/rest balance and general conduct were contained in the small yellow book that he issued each man with when he signed them, Buckley had a particular view on half-time refreshment for his team. He disliked players having a cup of tea, believing that it would lie heavy on their stomachs in the second half of a game and did little to refresh them. Perhaps if this view had have caught on and become common culture, many irate managers today would have to find an alternative to teacups to throw around the dressing room when their team underperforms!

The small yellow book became famous and it was a well thought out part of the Major's strategy to get footballers to be not only 'professional' in the sense of being paid for what they did, but also 'professional' in their attitudes and public behaviour. The book was reissued at the start of each season so that rules, instructions and codes could be updated annually. The book belonging to a deaf and dumb reserve player called Readman, who was on Wolves' books in 1933, lists eighteen instructions in all. Many of these dealt with the times players were expected to make themselves available for club duties (e.g. 10 a.m. daily for training; forty-five minutes before a home match and fifteen minutes at the railway station prior to departure to an away fixture). It also instructed players on how to look after the kit they were responsible for (hang up jerseys, provide own 'splits' (shinpads) and keep them clean). Rule 11 states that smoking is 'strictly forbidden' on the day of a match and before training. The next rule bans any player going dancing after the Wednesday of each week and rule 13 bans any player from riding on a motorcycle at any time, presumably because of the danger of being involved in a road accident. In those days, before players had agents and representatives, the rules banned anyone (other than club officials) from the dressing room. To reinforce loyalty and club control, players were not allowed to write press articles without prior club scrutiny and approval. The final item was a general appeal to players to exhibit professional integrity:

> The Directors wish to point out the honourable place your Club occupies in the Game and request that every player assist in building up the tone of professional football generally.
>
> Everything possible will be done for your comfort and advancement and you are asked 'to play the game' in the correct spirit and to conform to the rules and regulations as laid down [signed Frank C. Buckley].

The Major reinforced his rules and expectations with a system of fines for unacceptable behaviour on the part of players. Don Bilton recalls that players were fined 10s from their wages if they were five minutes late for training. This may be seen as a huge stoppage considering what a player was paid at the time, but Frank Buckley had no qualms about imposing such a fine. After all, he argued, at the time of signing them, he had given each player 'five bob to buy a good watch to get here on time'. Buckley's approach to dealing with players was quite revolutionary at the time and indicates much about his fresh ideas on management.

Frank Buckley was always proud of his own fitness and believed in leading by example. Even at the age of sixty-nine, when making a point to a Leeds player named Bobby Forrest about his fitness, he kicked high against a wall leaving a mark. The Major asked Forrest (who was almost a half-century younger) 'if I could reach it with my foot – and I couldn't!' The Major knew that players who were as fit as possible would not only perform better but would recover from injury a lot quicker than they might if they were unfit. He also sought players who were versatile and flexible enough to play in a variety of positions, although he knew they would gravitate to a 'natural' playing role for which they were best suited. Hence Billy Wright started off as a winger but became a great centre-back, and John Charles could play at centre forward or centre half. Buckley believed in developing upper-body strength in his players well before many clubs had addressed anything but ball skills in their players. Great use was made of very heavy medicine balls and weight training. Indeed, one of his initial actions at Wolves had been to persuade the directors to allow him to build a gymnasium at the ground. Such a facility was established under the Waterloo Road Stand by the Christmas of his first year in charge. The Major was not afraid of trying different methods to improve players' skills and performance. He not only encouraged Billy Wright to take up dancing but even employed a dancing master to instruct all his players in his time at Wolves. John Charles said that Buckley used the same approach at Leeds, when he held dance classes at training sessions on the Elland Road pitch. As this was still in the days when people danced in pairs, some of the taller players ended up with small wingers. The intent of instilling poise, balance and co-ordination into the men was often lost on them. Sadly, the whole exercise was seen as 'a bloody comedy act' by players such as Harold Williams.

Buckley used training methods that might now be seen as crude forms of psychological behaviour modification. At times his players trained with footballs considerably heavier than the standard weight, so that in a match the ball would feel lighter and easier to control. Considering the weight of match footballs in those days, these training balls must have weighed a ton! Players sometimes had a ball tied to one of their feet so that they were constantly practising dribbling and ball skills as they moved around the training ground. Footballers were taught to strike a ball effectively by having one placed on house bricks. If the ball was not hit properly, the player's shin or foot would painfully strike the bricks. One Leeds player was off for a week after mis-hitting the ball during this routine.

Wolves gymnasium, c. 1930.

Frank Buckley came into football management at a time of change and he knew that the public associated the team's performance with him. He saw the dressing room as a very manly place, more of a barrack room than a sporting facility. He was not averse to using very strong language and publicly lambasting and humiliating players he thought were not pulling their weight. At half-time in one game he turned on Charlie Phillips, a real star of the Wolves team, and went at him 'like a steam-roller without a driver'. Also, the Major was not averse to using sarcasm to drive home his point. He is reported as telling one hapless centre forward after a particularly inept performance, 'Jesus Christ was a clever man, but if he'd have played football he would never have found you!' Buckley's sarcasm could also be used to belittle the opposition. Cyril Sidlow recalls the Major referring to an Aston Villa centre forward as being 'like a dog running around a desert looking for a tree to pee up!' Even when he was an old man at Leeds he gave players his opinion of them while sitting in the stands, using a megaphone. At one session the Major was telling the unfortunate Bobby Forrest that he was 'f——ing useless' when local residents complained about the language. The Leeds directors took his megaphone away!

At whichever club he was at, to his players Major Buckley was not only their manager; he was their coach and trainer. Above all, he was the boss! For example, in 1938, a Manchester City player called Peter Dougherty had come into Molineux to visit his brother John, who was on Wolves' books. Thinking little of it and that he was doing no harm, he made his way down towards the changing room where he had been told to meet his brother. Apparently Buckley heard him on the famous marble floor and came out of his office. After the Major had berated him for being on the grounds without permission, Peter Dougherty said he 'was left in no doubt as to who ran Wolverhampton Wanderers!'

Buckley wasn't just concerned with his players' physical state. He knew that they must to be in the right frame of mind if matches were to be won. Jim Clayton, who played for Wolves between 1933 and 1938, and who the Major described as 'a grand centre forward' went through a barren period when he was unable to score. Every striker seems to experience such a lean period and, not surprisingly, Clayton started to get barracked by the Molineux faithful. Clayton became very depressed and was about to give up the game, and did in fact join the police force. The Major was very concerned about this and said that he feared 'a first-team football tragedy'. The Major tried to enthuse Clayton with the self-confidence that he lacked, but this was to no avail. After discussing the matter with his wife Dorothy, she suggested a course of psychology. As there were no specialists in this field at that time, Buckley contacted a local doctor who agreed to talk to the player. After half-a-dozen meetings with Clayton, the doctor went to Frank Buckley and excitedly insisted, 'Put him in the first team at once. Whatever happens Clayton must play this week.' The Major did as the doctor requested and Jim Clayton scored. He continued to score on a regular basis and found the net 14 times in the next 15 matches. One of the directors asked Buckley what had caused the turnaround in Clayton's performance. 'Psychology!' the Major replied. 'Codology, you mean,' the director laughed.

A few weeks later the player himself gave his perspective on his counselling treatment. In a letter to Dorothy Buckley, Jim Clayton wrote:

> I just learnt that it was you who was actually responsible for my treatment. I am very pleased with my success so far and I know you will be equally pleased. I cannot really thank you enough for what you have done. It must have been an inspiration. As you no doubt know the very name of Wolverhampton Wanderers was a nightmare to me. I detested the place. I do not think I was liked or respected by

a single person with the exception of Major Buckley, who I have no doubt was always interested in my welfare, even though I must have exasperated him often. I tried to escape by joining the Police Force, but it was no good. My heart was in football and I determined to try again. It was all to no purpose however and again I was a failure. Then came your inspiration.

It is quite rare to get the recipient's view of one of the Major's more controversial methods. Obviously it had saved Clayton's career and, more importantly, his mental health. It must be remembered that this was decades before others considered psychology, and it wasn't until 1958 that the Brazil World Cup team famously employed a psychologist's services. Buckley was obviously open-minded enough to try something new, but other players subsequently refused such therapy, confusing it with psychiatric treatment given to the mentally ill. All the same, one player later declared that he 'only had one more visit to make to the psychologist, then I will be cured!'

Major Buckley believed that ideally players should not be married. There was no sinister reason for this, but he did think that wives might 'get in the way' of players concentrating on developing their skills. Whereas a wife's anxieties about her husband's safety might affect him and his performance, it would not be a consideration if the player were single. Major Buckley had forty players in his 1937 squad and all were bachelors!

Frank Buckley was very clear on the style of play that he wanted to see on the pitch. His 'game plans' were simple and unfussy. Buckley believed in what Stan Cullis later called 'the direct method of playing', although critics since have sneeringly condemned it as 'kick and rush'. Buckley and Cullis meant that close inter-passing and square-ball play were done away with and replaced by long, across-field passing. It was simply the task of the defenders to get the ball forward as quickly as possible and not to over-elaborate their roles. The wingers were to take opposition defenders on and cross the ball to the central attackers whose job it was to put the ball in the net. What could be simpler? Players were expected to do exactly as Major Buckley ordered, otherwise, as Cullis said, 'you'd very soon be on your bicycle to another club'. He wanted fewer dribbling moves and more passing. Buckley condemned footballers for hanging on too long and 'carrying' the ball far too much.

Major Buckley had a plethora of views on how players should have been treated by their clubs and the Football Association. In a series of articles he wrote in the mid-1950s, after he had retired from football, he outlined his views. At the time football players were still on a 'fixed' wage, although moves were afoot, championed by Fulham's Jimmy Hill, to have this practice abolished. Buckley believed that the fixed wage had led to a lot of corruption with illegal 'under the counter' payments made to players. Buckley proposed to scrap the fixed wage in favour of a sliding scale of payment according to the quality of the performance they had given. Exactly how each player's performance would have been assessed, or whether they would be judged on results alone, is unclear. He did not believe in 'win bonuses' because, as he said, 'Why pay a man for winning when that is what he is supposed to do?' He believed that players should be on five-year contracts, and that loyalty bonuses should be paid out to players only when they finally hung their boots up.

Frank Buckley knew that a man's playing career was relatively short and that football should provide him with the means of earning a living after he had ceased to play. So long as a 'lad had ability, a small-sized, level head and a liking for hard work', his football career could serve as the foundation for a secure future. Major Buckley would cite the case of George Ashall, an ex-colliery worker who, in a little over a season playing for Wolves, made enough money to buy a partnership in a thriving fruit and vegetable business. Ashall, according to the Major, succeeded because 'he was not afraid of hard work'. Buckley admired such men and could not stand the idle. He once stated: 'The fellow who stands around the changing room with his hands in his pockets is no use to me, the club or himself.'

Buckley was always trying to find ways of giving his players an advantage – an 'edge', as it were – that might swing the match in their favour. If it wasn't specifically banned or illegal, the Major was willing to have a go. It became quite well known in the late 1930s that Major Buckley would have the Molineux pitch flooded. The Buckley 'Babes' had trained on very wet pitches and so were used to the water-logged conditions. Of course opponents weren't and were soon at a disadvantage. One T. G. Jones of Everton describes going to Molineux to play and finding it 'a sea of mud' even though there had been no rain for ages. He went on, 'We were on our bottoms more than our feet, to be honest.' It was the Everton trainer who, upon inspecting the Wolves' pitch prior to a game, had almost to beg Buckley on bended knee for the key to the boot room so the boots of the Toffeemen could be fitted with longer studs to deal with the wet pitch. Everton soon after successfully sought a ruling from the FA banning the over-watering of pitches during the wetter months of the football season.

Cartoon highlighting the effects of Buckley having the Molineux pitch watered.

A more significant ruse used by Buckley was the infamous 'monkey-gland treatment' he introduced to Molineux in the late summer of 1937. Sometime earlier in the season, Major Buckley had been approached by a chemist called Menzies Sharp who had a 'secret remedy that would give [the] players confidence'. Although sceptical at first because he had 'often been button-holed by quacks wishing to sell me everything from charms to witch doctors' recipes', the Major was impressed by Sharp. He agreed to try it out with his players, of whom only two refused. Billy Wright agreed but later claimed to have given his dose to his landlady's tomcat. Apparently the tom became very popular with all the female cats in the neighbourhood!

The 'gland treatment' was a course of twelve injections for each man, prepared by Menzies Sharp. The treatment was administered by Dick Bradford, who was the Wolves' trainer. There were to be two courses per season and, although the Major wished to keep it a secret, word soon got out. He was forced to make a public statement on the matter. 'We are experimenting with the treatment and it is difficult to say what the results will be until it has been continued for some time,' he said. 'I have great faith in it and we are hopeful of making our young players stronger.' Wolves were subjected to a great deal of derision shortly afterwards when Arsenal beat them 5-0. Buckley was condemned for 'doping-up' his players and even the secretary of the Players' Union went to press to attack him, but he was adamant he was doing nothing untoward. He later wrote about it:

> Gland treatment was not a course of drugs, it was a treatment that could be broken off at any time and there were no ill effects. We are all lacking something, or else have a superfluity in one or more glands. To be perfectly fit all glands must be balanced. It follows that any treatment must be individual. You cannot go to a shop and buy a bottle of

gland pills and know that you have got a perfect tonic. To be honest, I was rather sceptical about this treatment and thought it best to try it out on myself first. The treatment lasted three or four months. Long before it was over I felt so much benefit that I asked the players if they would be willing to undergo it and that is how the gland treatment became general at Molineux. The youngsters were treated and careful measurements taken. The speed of their physical measurements was amazing. I do not know of a single ill effect. No sane person would suggest that glands or any other treatment would make a footballer out of an individual, but properly administered by a competent authority it can be of great benefit.

Despite this statement that the treatment was voluntary, the vast majority of his players were cajoled by into taking the treatment by Buckley. The two players who were known to have refused were Dickie Dorsett and Don Bilton. Dorsett, a well-established and experienced footballer, had stood up to Major Buckley's insistence (some might say bullying) on a number of occasions. However, with Don Bilton, it was another matter entirely.

A pre-war cartoon showing the supposed effects of the 'monkey-gland treatment'.

Don Bilton had been signed in 1938 as a goalkeeper from York City. Major Buckley had such faith in his scouts that the seventeen-year-old Bilton was taken on by Wolves without Frank Buckley having seen him play. Don Bilton's father, a former professional goalkeeper himself, was then a commercial traveller. When Wolves signed his son, he moved his whole family to Wolverhampton. Don recalled his first day at the Waterloo Road club:

> It was a Friday and when I went into the Molineux Major Buckley stuck his head out of his office door and said, 'Who are you?' I told him my name and he said, 'Alright sonny. Report to the medical room on Monday for your gland injections.' I said, 'I'm sorry Sir, but I am only seventeen and still under my father's guidance. He will not want me to have injections.' Major Buckley told me I was under contract and I would do as I was told! I went home and told my father, who said, 'So that's what he said, did he! We'll see about that!' Father had fought in the Great War and was not to be messed about with.
>
> The following Monday I returned to the Molineux with my father and when the Major saw him he demanded, 'What's he doing here?' and told me to report to the medical room. My father told Buckley to get back into his office, which he did. My father followed him in and a fearful row ensued, with the two men standing toe to toe, their noses only inches apart. After a lot of shouting and 'soldierly swearing', the Major reluctantly conceded that I would not to have the monkey-gland treatment. Buckley was not at all pleased by this and I never did much good at Wolves after that!

After each game where players had received gland treatment, Wolves sent a report to both the League and the FA, who had suspicions of the treatment after Leicester City had lodged a complaint after being beaten 10-1 by Buckley's 'supermen'. There was even a question raised in the House of Commons on the matter by the Leicester MP, Montague Lyons. He asked the Minister of Health 'whether his attention had been directed to statements that that gland extracts from animals are being administered to football players... and whether he will order an investigation into those allegations, and whether he regards this practice as desirable in the interests of national health?' In reply, Walter Elliot, the Minister of Health, said he did not think an investigation was required, although Manny Shinwell, the famous Liverpool Labour MP, thought it might be a good idea to give glands to the Tory cabinet!

The famous pre-war football star Tommy Lawton was convinced Wolves played in a hypnotic trance bought on by the gland treatment. He said, 'When we went to Wolves, I saw Stan Cullis. I'd met him through being in the England side. "Hello, Stan," I said, and he walked past me with glazed eyes. There's no question they were on these monkey pills, they definitely were, and after they had licked us 7–0 I was sure they were.' Despite such a heavy loss, the Everton captain consoled his team by saying Wolves had the wind with them. 'Some wind!' Alex Stephenson said. Stan Cullis said the gland treatment was overplayed and never affected him so perhaps it was more a case of 'codology' with him and Lawton.

The controversy over the treatment rumbled on a while longer until, finding no case to answer, the Football League posted a circular in the dressing rooms of every club in England and Wales. This declared that players could take glands, but only on a voluntary basis. It may be coincidence, but both FA Cup finalists of 1939 used gland treatment, and little was made of this. However, it does show that others followed where Buckley had led. The whole business petered out during the war, although the Major made some attempt at reviving gland treatment while with Leeds. However, many of the players who had seen service in the Forces had had enough of injections. As one of their players, Harold Williams, eloquently put it, 'I don't require needles up my backside to play football.' Incidentally Major Buckley never referred to 'monkey' glands at all. The reference to primates came solely

Cartoons of the Wolves, late 1930s.

from the press. There had been talk of extracting bulls' glands for use on players, but it would be another fifty years before a 'Bull-inspired' team would turn out at Molineux – and that inspiration would be Steve Bull!

It is important to see the whole 'monkey gland' issue in its historical context. In the 1930s, when Menzies Sharp was extending the original experiments of French physiologists into the apparent beneficial effects on humans of glands extracted from an animal's testicles, he was reflecting widely held popular beliefs. The 'eugenics movement' of the early twentieth century believed that the physical qualities of human beings could be predicted by experimentally analysing the attributes of people's forebears. This approach was taken to a sinister and evil extent by the Nazi rulers of Germany who experimented on prisoners in concentration camps in their search for a super-fit and pure 'Aryan race'. Even in America there was huge interest in people who would be far fitter and more active than the average man or woman. There it was to manifest itself in media fantasy with advent of comic book heroes such as 'Superman'.

Major Buckley was always open to new ideas, like the gland treatment, in the hope that they could improve the performance of his players. He was always thinking up novel ideas. Cameron Buchanan said being at the Molineux of the time was 'like being in the laboratory of some mad professor' as there were so many new ideas being tried. Before one match Major Buckley left several bottles of whisky on the table in the changing room. The players thought that they were in for some memorable post-match celebrations. When Buckley came in they were instructed to rub the spirit into their legs like embrocation. When the team were subsequently beaten, one of the players described the Major's experiment as 'a bloody good waste of whisky'. In 1938, he readily tried out a 'football firing machine' that was being hawked around the grounds of the more famous First Division clubs. The contraption was used to help train Alex Scott the goalkeeper, but it never caught on. Buckley had invited Pathé News to film the Wolves training with the machine. Soon it was being shown at cinemas throughout the country (alongside items on the deteriorating international situation), between the 'B' film and the main feature. The Major would be pleased about this. He had a good eye for publicity, as the following story illustrates.

In the mid-1930s a man called Walter E. Turner farmed at Chapel Ash Farm in Paget Road off the Tettenhall Road in Wolverhampton, at a site now occupied by Wolverhampton College. It seems that Mr Turner had spent three days in Wales buying sheep for his farm. They were delivered by train to Great Western sidings in Herbert Street near Wolverhampton's Low Level Station. Mr Turner collected the flock from here late one evening shortly afterwards. As he drove his sheep through the town towards Compton, a heavy fog descended, Mr Turner happened to meet Frank Buckley who asked where he was taking the sheep. Mr Turner explained. Major Buckley told him to put the sheep on the Molineux pitch overnight. The weather was worsening and there was a danger of losing some of the animals. Mr Turner gratefully accepted the Major's offer and the gates of the Molineux were opened to admit this somewhat different crowd. The next day the weather had cleared and Mr Turner returned to Molineux to collect his flock. In the meantime, Major Buckley had contacted the *Express and Star* and a photograph of the sheep on the pitch was published in that night's edition of the paper. It is not certain whether or not the sheep became ardent Wolves fans after their free entry to Molineux. It is more likely they would have supported Derby County who, after all, are called 'The Rams'!

Such publicity stunts increased Buckley's personal fame and made people stop and listen to his views on a range of issues relating to football. Many of his ideas on the organisation of the sport and the part football played in the wider social context were well ahead of their time. Major Buckley believed that there should have been a Great Britain football team on the same lines as other sporting teams appearing in the Olympics. This idea never came to fruition as the relative strength of home nations' teams in the islands where the game was first developed was thought to give them an advantage over other countries. The concept has never gone away and has been discussed on numerous occasions ever since. He certainly foresaw a European league for the better teams from each of the European nations – Major Buckley was talking about this in the 1930s. The European Champions' League is now well established, but Buckley thought this out over half a century before it was realised.

The Major saw football not only in terms of a sport, but also as an entertainment. In the 1920s he foresaw a time when all paying customers would arrive at an all-seater football ground prior to a match and dine in one of many luxurious restaurants to be found there before taking their place under cover to enjoy the game. He thought that even local grounds would be the same size as the Empire Stadium at Wembley with a capacity of 100,000 spectators. In fact, Major Buckley had promoted the idea of moving Wolves from Molineux to such a 'super ground' at Compton Park on the outskirts of the town. He argued that not only would ample land be available for a much bigger stadium, but the support facilities such as a railway line for travelling fans were already in place nearby. Stan Cullis also promoted this idea in the 1950s when he managed Wolves. More recently, Wolves have built training facilities on the stadium site Major Buckley had in mind.

Buckley thought there was a place for multi-sport use of grounds, and he tried to support boxing promotions at the Molineux. In 1937 he gave active support to a request from a boxing promoter for a welterweight contest between Jack Kilrain from Glasgow and locally born Charlie Baxter. It was intended the fight should take place at the ground during the first week in July to coincide with the Royal Show. However, the Wolves directors expressed reservations about the proposals and the fight did not take place. The idea was not to disappear completely as boxing became a regular event in the 1950s.

In the 1920s both Herbert Chapman and Frank Buckley advocated footballers wearing numbered shirts so that spectators could identify them from a distance. This idea was eventually adopted for the 1933 FA Cup final to help radio commentators identify players for the listening public. Both men always insisted that they were the first to promote the idea.

Major Buckley's vision of how football should be run included players staying overnight when playing distant away fixtures. The norm at the time was to travel to all venues on the day of the game, with players often arriving tired and fatigued. Buckley thought that where possible, players should be ferried to games by air and stated that by the 1950s every club should have its own helicopter to do this. He also believed players would benefit from playing abroad and advocated annual trips to Europe.

Frank Buckley's greatest talent was undoubtedly his ability to spot and nurture young talented players. He wanted to develop this further and foresaw the establishment of players' academies for young lads. He almost succeeded in this while at Wolves. In 1938 the club bought a large detached property in the Penn area of the town, called Ireton Lodge. Major Buckley's plan was to demolish this building, which had originally been built by a former Mayor of Wolverhampton named John Jones in the late nineteenth century. In its place 'a building on up-to-date hotel lines' would be erected. Buckley had been given a budget of between £12,000 and £16,000 to pay for the new building, which would contain a gym, a physiotherapy room, tennis and squash courts and a putting green as well as a dining room and fourteen bedrooms. Sadly, the players' hotel was never built because all plans were put on hold when the Second World War broke out. The idea wasn't taken up after the war.

Frank Buckley was able to see a much bigger social and commercial picture in which football played a significant part. As early as 1927 he made a speech at the Victoria Hotel near Wolverhampton's railway station. He told his audience, 'Football is a business, a prestige has to be maintained. A football club in a town is an asset. It brings people to it and benefits the Corporation through patronage of tramcars and increased business for tradespeople.' It was important that a council understood that its local football club should be valued and supported (it was reckoned that industrial production rose ten per cent in the town in the week following a Wolves win). Major Buckley advocated that local authorities should own football grounds. This would not only ensure their economic survival, but would also limit the influence of directors. Buckley had a lot of experience of club directors and often found them wanting. He believed that involving local government would bring some of the checks and balances of local democracy to the sport. On a level up from this, he hoped for a Ministry of Sport. This ambition was realised some years later.

Ireton Lodge.

Despite being a non-smoker and only a moderate drinker, Major Buckley was no prude. He understood that people liked to gamble and wrote that the tote should operate within grounds and profits should go to the clubs. He also said that the football pools, which emerged in the 1930s as the main weekly 'flutter' of a lot of Britons, should be run and controlled by the Football League. He resented private companies making vast amounts out of his beloved sport, but the League did not feel suitably competent to take up this suggestion, as running pools would be outside their usual area of interest.

The Major at his desk.

All in all, Franklin Charles Buckley was a unique character in the annals of British football. Without Buckley, Wolves would not have become the famous club it was in the 1950s. He came to a club in debt and left them nearly eighteen years later having made a massive £110,000 for Wolves in transfer dealings. Even though he had moved on by 1949, Wolves' FA Cup-winning team of that year had no less than seven players who had been signed by the Major, and were indeed the basis of the fabulous Wolves teams of the 1950s. Stan Cullis was the first to admit his debt to Buckley who taught him to be a footballer, captain, and finally a manager.

The Major has been described as a maverick, an enigma, a character and, above all, a genius – maybe he was. Perhaps Eddie Holding best summed up the Major's lasting influence:

'They ought to put a statue up to Major Buckley just outside the Molineux, and then put those of Billy Wright and Stan Cullis just behind it.

After all, he was the first and they followed in his wake.'

Other titles published by Tempus

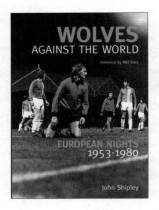

Wolves Against the World European Nights 1953-1980
JOHN SHIPLEY

The 1950s saw Wolverhampton Wanderers take on the best teams from Europe and the rest of the world under the Molineux floodlights. Classic encounters in the European Champions' Cup and European Cup-Winners' Cup were followed by UEFA Cup, Anglo-Italian Cup and Texaco Cup ties in the 1960s, '70s and '80s. Capturing the true spirit of the time, this book recounts those memorable nights and the great players and exciting football of the Wolves in their glory years.

0 7524 2947 7

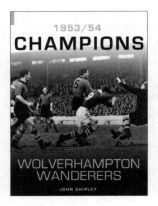

Wolverhampton Wanderers Champions 1953/54
JOHN SHIPLEY

In 1953/54 Wolverhampton Wanderers won their first ever League Championship: the first of a hat-trick of titles they were to win in the fabulous fifties. This is the story of that incredible campaign, recounted game by game, as Wolves successfully fought off a concerted challenge from arch-rivals West Bromwich Albion. Each match is described in thrilling detail, once again bringing to life the great players of the era and evoking a time when Wolves were the best team in England.

0 7524 3234 6

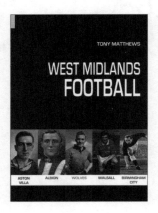

West Midlands Football
TONY MATTHEWS

Focusing on five clubs – Aston Villa, Birmingham City, West Bromwich Albion, Wolverhampton Wanderers and Walsall – this is the story of League and cup football in the West Midlands. This part of England has seen no small amount of footballing success, with League Championships, FA Cups, League Cups and European honours being won by West Midlands clubs. The great players and passionately fought local derbies are recounted here in a fine illustrated history that is sure to delight all fans.

0 7524 3270 2

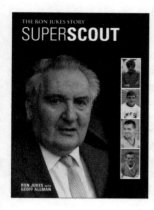

Superscout The Ron Jukes Story

RON JUKES WITH GEOFF ALLMAN

In a long and distinguished career, Ron Jukes has brought to light the talents of many young players. Serving Wolves, Walsall and Derby County among others as chief scout, his discoveries have included the England internationals Allan Clarke, Phil Parkes and Steve Bull. In this, his autobiography, Ron tells of the hours he has spent soaked to the skin watching park football and of some of the unusual circumstances in which he has signed players. This is the story of one of football's unsung heroes.

0 7524 3070 X

Walsall Football Club

GEOFF ALLMAN

The images in this book capture over 100 years of Walsall's history, encompassing glory days and heartaches, giant-killing feats and plucky promotion campaigns. It features players who went on to become household names, such as England strikers Dennis Wilshaw and Allan Clarke, and also less well-known characters who have nonetheless battled heroically to keep the club alive. This superb pictorial history will appeal to Walsall fans of all ages.

0 7524 2091 7

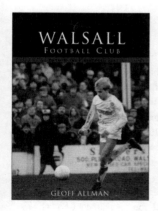

Walsall Football Club Classics Fifty of the Finest Matches
GEOFF ALLMAN

In this book, Walsall Football Club historian Geoff Allman looks at fifty of the Saddlers' classic games, helping fans to relive the great moments of their club's history – from performing giant-killing acts against Arsenal and Manchester United in the FA Cup to winning against the odds and maintaining their Division One status. It recounts Walsall's highs and lows, reminiscing about the goals, the saves, the skills and the heart-warming displays that make football the game it is.

0 7524 2432 7

Leeds United Football Club

DAVID SAFFER & HOWARD DAPIN

This selection of over 200 images, including action shots, team line-ups, player portraits, programme covers and cartoons, follows the club from its foundation in 1919 up to the end of the twentieth century. Included along the way are many special events, such as the Fairs Cup triumphs in 1968 and 1971, the League Championships of 1968/69, 1973/74 and 1991/92 and the 1972 FA Cup. Anyone with an interest in the club will love this collection, which celebrates the tradition of excellence that belongs to Leeds United.

0 7524 1642 1

Leeds Legends

DAVID SAFFER

Hundreds of players have worn the shirt of Leeds United with pride over the decades. From loyal club stalwarts to controversial mavericks, many have attained legendary status at Elland Road, and this book celebrates some of the men most prominent in the club's history. Over 100 great names are featured in *Leeds Legends*, including stars of the famous promotion, championship and cup-winning sides. The book contains biographies, illustrations, statistics and a foreword by the late, great John Charles CBE.

0 7524 2700 8

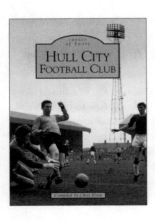

Hull City Football Club

CHRIS ELTON

Hull City FC has a long history of which its fans can be proud. This book illustrates that history with over 200 images tracing the Tigers' story from the foundation of the club in 1904 to the end of the twentieth century. Highlights include the 1930 FA Cup semi-final, the divisional championships in 1932/33, 1948/49 and 1965/66 and the Associate Members' Cup final in 1984. Numerous promotion and relegation seasons are also featured, as are many of the great players to have represented the Tigers.

0 7524 1620 0

If you are interested in purchasing other books published by Tempus, or in case you have difficulty finding any Tempus books in your local bookshop, you can also place orders directly through our website

www.tempus-publishing.com